STILL FLYING

A Celebration of Joss Whedon's Acclaimed Television Series

CONTRIBUTIONS FROM
BEN EDLUND
JANE ESPENSON
BRETT MATTHEWS
JOSE MOLINA

FEATURES AND INTERVIEWS BY
TARA BENNETT
ABBIE BERNSTEIN
KARL DERRICK

TITAN BOOKS

VISIT HISTORIC

SERENITY VALLEY

NATIONAL PARK

宁静
ALRICH

STILL FLYING

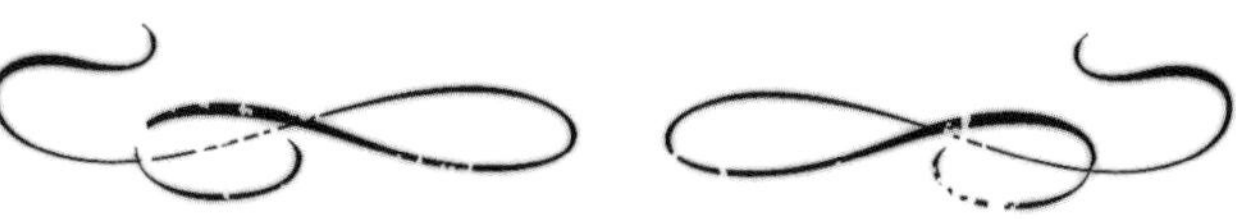

FIREFLY: STILL FLYING

ISBN 9781848565067

Published by Titan Books, a division of
Titan Publishing Group Ltd.
144 Southwark Street
London
SE1 0UP

First edition May 2010
2 4 6 8 10 9 7 5 3 1

Firefly: Still Flying
A Celebration of Joss Whedon's Acclaimed Television Series

Based on the series created by Joss Whedon.

Book designed by Martin Stiff, based on designs by Marcus Scudamore.
Production by Bob Kelly.

这本书是一个青日合作出版

What did you think of this book? We love to hear from our readers.
Please email us at: **readerfeedback@titanemail.com** or write to us at the above address.
You can also visit us at **www.titanbooks.com**

A CIP catalogue record for this title is available from the British Library.

Printed and bound in the USA.

CONTENTS

THE LEGACY OF FIREFLY

By Way of an Introduction...

❖ This page: On set during filming of the original pilot episode, 'Serenity'.

Simon: Are you always this sentimental?
Mal: Had a good day.
Simon: You had the Alliance on you, criminals and savages... half the people on the ship have been shot or wounded including yourself, and you're harboring known fugitives.
Mal: We're still flying.
Simon: That's not much.
Mal: It's enough.

FROM THE FIREFLY EPISODE '*SERENITY*', BY JOSS WHEDON

"*Firefly* was a family like I've never known. *Firefly* spoiled me rotten. You hope and dream that you will get a job where you get to go to work every day and say, "Oh my god – look what I get to do today! I kicked him in the engine!" You want to work with people that you really enjoy, and people whose work you can respect. You want to work with people, a crew, that every day not only wants to go to work and do their jobs well, and that are creative and capable, but also want to have a good time doing it. And are willing to sacrifice just to make it better and make it fun. I had that."

NATHAN FILLION, SPEAKING ON STAGE AT THE 'STARFURY' CONVENTION, 2004

"The *Firefly* fans – the Browncoats – the charity work they've done remains extremely important to me and sort of stunning, and they themselves have become enough of an industry myth – a legend, I should say – that they make people think that my fanbase is much bigger than it actually is. I think they've helped other projects of mine, because people see that the revenue stream is about the long haul and not the opening weekend. These people have also proved that fans are not just people who chase actors around, but they're also people who form communities and help people for the joy of doing it. They have done as much as any group I know to change the face of fandom. I'm not entirely sure I deserve them, but I ain't giving them up."

JOSS WHEDON, INTERVIEW WITH ABBIE BERNSTEIN, 2009

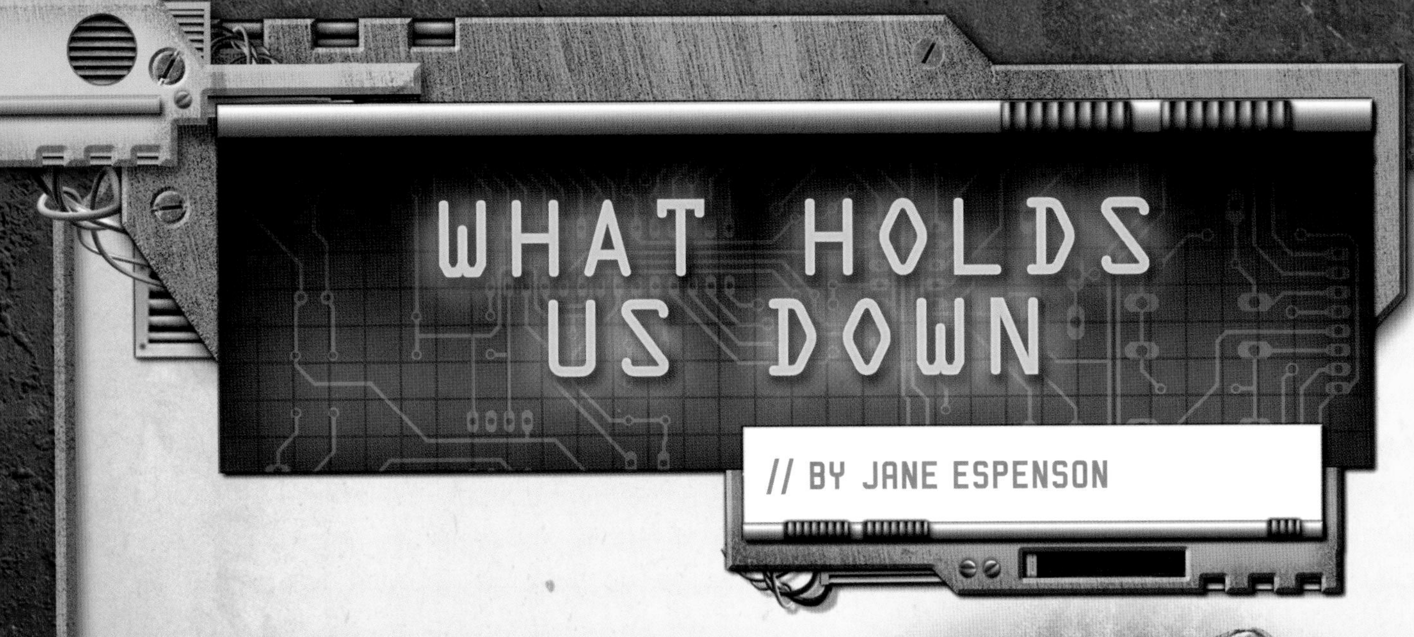

WHAT HOLDS US DOWN

// BY JANE ESPENSON

Kaylee's hands were shaking. They had blood on them, too, not so much under the nails, but around the edges. A' course, she didn't need steady right yet. She needed strong. Later, if there was a later, the blood would wash clean. There was wordplay in there somewhere. Wash's blood.

Plan had been to break into this floating junkyard and steal replacement parts for her girl Serenity. Money was tight and supplies were thin and the place was run by Bad Guys anyway, guys who stole ships off humble smugglers. Only it turned out that the Bad Guys were smarter than they'd made provision for and now Wash was dying and Kaylee was hurt and Serenity had flown away without them. And now she and Wash were on this scrapped Series One Firefly they'd found in the yard. The ship felt a little like home but not at all *really* like home.

The deck plate was awful heavy. She wiped her hands on her coveralls, the teddy-bear patch taking the worst of it, and she reached for the incised handhold again. But the plates were gummed into place, held fast by their own weight and the grime of years — coagulated oil and, in places, the droppings of the scrapyard rats. She'd seen some dead rats in the corners of the hold already, a few inside the radiation shielding, too — a bad place to nest, even in a dead ship. Rats are none too bright on the best of days.

She tried to ignore the pained noises that Wash was making as she got the edge of a plate lifted up and jammed a wedge under it. It felt not quite right to listen to someone's pain like that. He wasn't properly awake, neither, which made it even more private.

She made a lever, *Simple machines for simple people*, she recited in her mind, only slightly hysterically.

The Bad Guys had to be searching for them.

Her plan was going to require time and she was pretty sure time was something they had none of. Then she was sliding the plate aside. She had to go slow, since the metal on metal of it made a *skreel* noise that had her aching head beating like a drum and would surely bring the Bad Guys arunning if they heard it.

Wash woke up from the noise and his eyes were wide and scared. They made Kaylee's heart hurt. They both waited, holding their breath, listening for running footsteps and shouts that would mean they'd been discovered. They didn't hear anything, but that didn't mean too much. They might be Crepe-Soled Bad Guys. She hadn't really noticed.

She pulled Wash down into the opening between decks, carefully gripping him, neck-and-side, then ass-and-legs as she eased his lower half down, trying to be unaware of his body under her hands, trying to pretend there wasn't something awful in the intimacy. He hissed from the pain. More blood got on her hands, mixing with the oil and grime from the deck.

They were under the deck, now. It was dark and hot and full of massive grav dampeners. If she hadn't already known this ship was dead, she'd've known because down was still down here. If the grav dampeners were working, then the gravity underdeck would've been opposite and they'd've been pulled up toward the underside of the deck plating. Instead, down remained down, meaning that the gravity of the floating junkyard was still king here. She knelt on the subfloor. The rats down here weren't quite as

dead and she heard them skittering. Kaylee had to figure rat-dancing as the least of their problems.

She hauled Wash as far astern in the ship as she could get him, bumping him over and under obstacles 'tween decks, her hands under his sweaty pits, his heels kicking at the subfloor as he tried to help push himself along. When she was exhausted and he was more or less unconscious again from the pain, she left him and made her way back to the treasure chests — to the dampeners.

The damps were big, a' course, taller than she was. She lifted open the metal shielding at the bottom of the first damp, exposing the control assembly. There, held in a big clamp like a fig in a baby's hand was a short, fat rod with copper rings around it. That was a honey, and that was what she needed. They were Honnecourt Capacitors, but everyone just called them honeys. It took a little muscle work to pull 'em, but she worked her way down the line, trying to be quiet and fast. She fashioned a leather strap into something like a bandolier and tucked them into that, crossways to her body. But even then, five was as many as she could carry. She crawled her way back to Wash, listening for people outside the ship, even though she wasn't sure she'd hear 'em until it was too late.

Series One Fireflies were rare as hen's lips and it wasn't often you'd get to play in one. A' course, it would be better if Wash wasn't wheezing now, making a very slight bubbling noise that she hated with her whole being. She sat down next to him and started working on the rods. These were set to work in the damps, making it so the contents of the ship didn't float around. She needed 'em to work in the rotor, so they'd make

the ship able to resist the pull of the junkyard's own gravity system. It required some math and some guesswork, but she figured she was as apt to get it right as anyone was, which wasn't very, but worth a shot. It would make for a hell of a bothersome ride, but escapers can't be choosers.

"Hey, Wash? You're not sleeping there, are you?"

"Me? No way. I'm dying. No time to sleep."

"You're not dying."

"No? I'll show you."

"Shut up." Then, after a moment's thought, she added, "Keep talking."

She heard definite footsteps then, from outside the ship. From right below, sounded like. And voices. Men, saying things like "Back half a' the yard's clear." and "Look over there." She locked eyes with Wash until the voices faded.

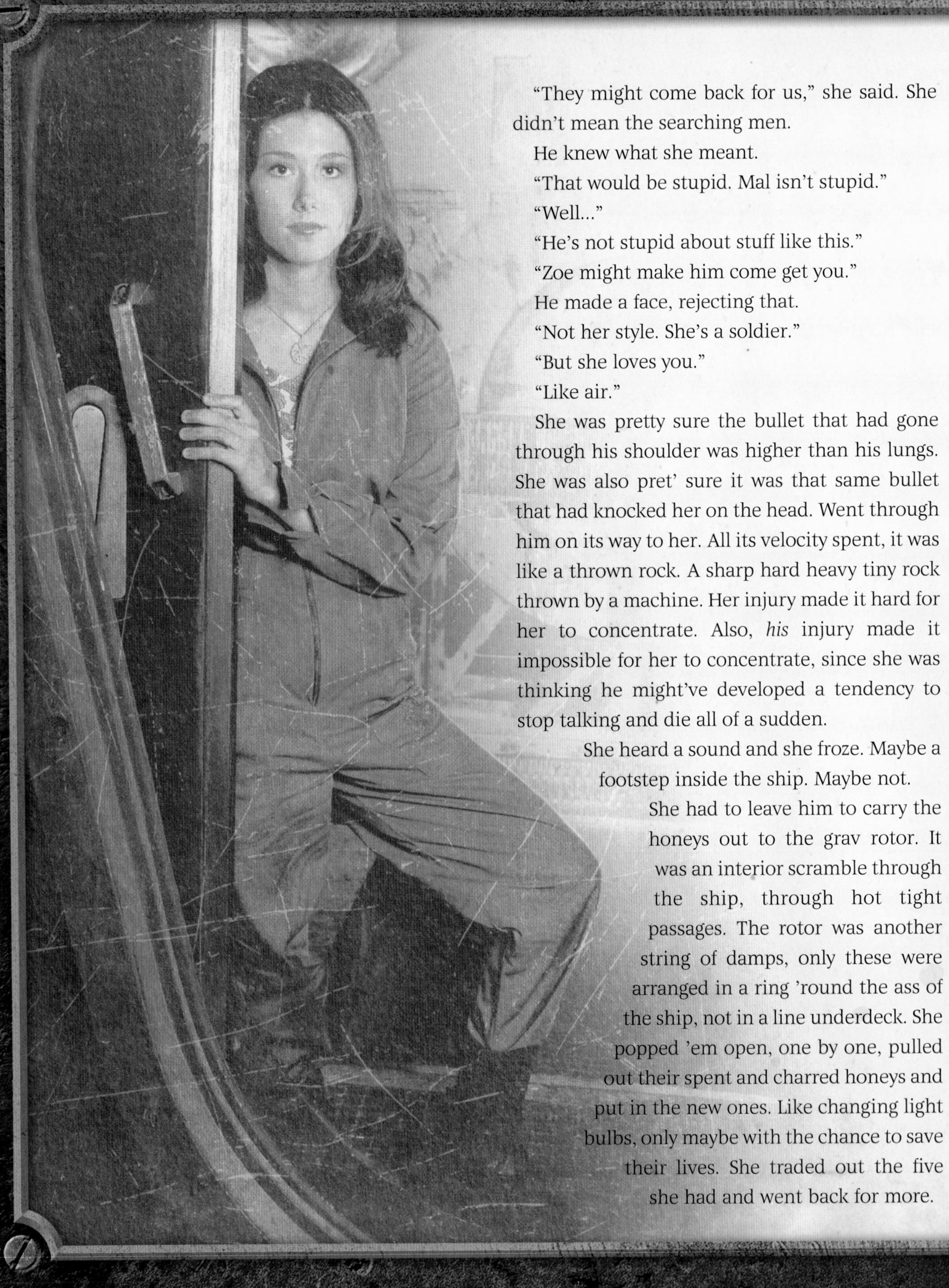

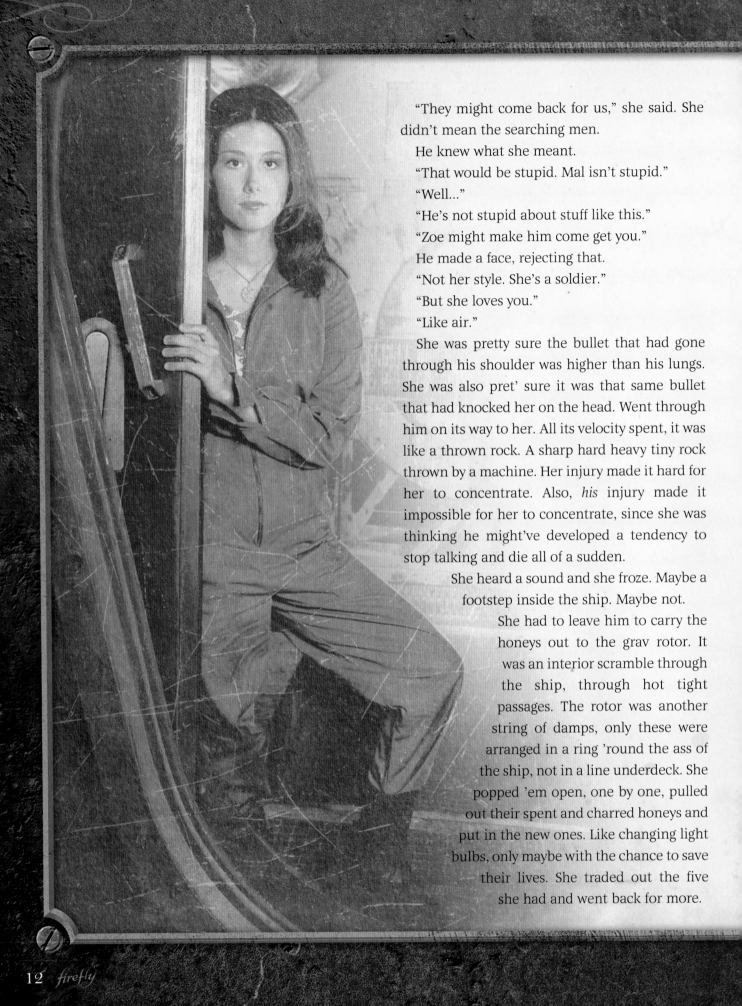

"They might come back for us," she said. She didn't mean the searching men.

He knew what she meant.

"That would be stupid. Mal isn't stupid."

"Well..."

"He's not stupid about stuff like this."

"Zoe might make him come get you."

He made a face, rejecting that.

"Not her style. She's a soldier."

"But she loves you."

"Like air."

She was pretty sure the bullet that had gone through his shoulder was higher than his lungs. She was also pret' sure it was that same bullet that had knocked her on the head. Went through him on its way to her. All its velocity spent, it was like a thrown rock. A sharp hard heavy tiny rock thrown by a machine. Her injury made it hard for her to concentrate. Also, *his* injury made it impossible for her to concentrate, since she was thinking he might've developed a tendency to stop talking and die all of a sudden.

She heard a sound and she froze. Maybe a footstep inside the ship. Maybe not.

She had to leave him to carry the honeys out to the grav rotor. It was an interior scramble through the ship, through hot tight passages. The rotor was another string of damps, only these were arranged in a ring 'round the ass of the ship, not in a line underdeck. She popped 'em open, one by one, pulled out their spent and charred honeys and put in the new ones. Like changing light bulbs, only maybe with the chance to save their lives. She traded out the five she had and went back for more.

Every time she passed Wash, he'd wake up and look at her like he was surprised. He was a little less there every time. She sat down next to him with another bunch of honeys and set about adjusting them.

She thought about Simon and how she would feel if he was gone. Like she couldn't breathe. Like air. She didn't want to think about that.

"Hey, Wash. I can fix this ship, but I can't fly it."

He opened his eyes, which surprised her a little. For a minute he'd been more landscape than person. He grinned, then looked like he regretted it.

"You make this pile of *gou shi* fly and I'll pilot it."

"It's not a pile of *gou shi.* "

He moved a hand and pointed at something.

Kaylee looked and then smiled.

"It has piles of *gou shi in it.* Not the same thing."

He closed his eyes and she felt colder.

She heard the footsteps and the voices more often now outside the ship. That meant they were working a search grid. Sooner or later, this ship, this hulk among the other hulks, would be searched.

"What are you doing?" He coughed after he asked the question, but she ignored it.

"Fixing it."

"How?"

"Moving the gravity around."

"Well, of course."

She crawled to the grav rotor again. A five-minute trip there. Then ten minutes to get the honeys into place. Then five minutes back, her bandolier empty. Sometimes she'd hear Wash coughing before she got to him. That made her worry because sound carried. The times when she didn't hear him made her worry more. She pulled the last batch of honeys and sat next to him again.

"Does it bother you? About Mal and Zoe?"

"What?"

The way he said "What?" was all drifty and unsure, as if what he meant was "What are you and why are you standing between me and the vivid blue peace that is death?" So she set a honey on the sub-deck *hard*, so it made noise, and she asked again, more loudly:

"Does it bother you that her first loyalty is to him?"

He went "Huh," at that. A little irked, which struck her as shiny. Seemed to her a man couldn't die with irk in him.

"Does it?"

"She loves me helplessly."

"Mal's a hero. Coat and hair and tight pants and big ol' shoulders with no holes in them."

"You're provoking me."

"Ain't I though?"

"This hurts." It was the first time he'd talked about pain. She didn't like it.

"Why in the whole 'verse does Zoe love you, Wash?"

"I'm funny."

"Really? I'd love to hear that some time."

"I'm good in bed."

"Not what she told me." This was a lie. Zoe had said he was good. She'd used gestures.

"I'm cute."

"Not at the moment. Gotta say, I'm finding this to be an enduring mystery."

After a while, he said, "She loves me because I love her for the right reasons."

"Clearly nonsense."

"Well, yes."

The work with the honeys had become

automatic. Kaylee carried the last ones out through the hot cramped obstacle course of the ship and returned. She crouched and touched his non-holey shoulder and asked him, "Got an answer yet?"

He didn't answer for a while, but finally he said, "I'm a carrier."

"What? Like for a disease?"

"Yeah. I don't suffer from heroism, but everyone around me does, so I figure I'm a carrier."

"Zoe was a big damn war hero before you even knew her..."

"'S retroactive." His voice sort of sank over the horizon and she hoped he was just asleep.

All the honeys had been moved, so she went back and faced the grav rotor. Looking at the big exterior spinning ring from the inside, while it wasn't spinning, made it hard to figure out if this was going to work. She couldn't turn anything on, run any power through the system without calling the attention of the still-circling Bad Guys to them. So she sat and stared and played a game she liked to call "Kaylee is an electron" in which she traced the interior mechanism in her head. She found a half-dozen places to be concerned. Parts to check, connections to verify. But a voice rang out, way too close – "Did anyone check the Firefly?"

She raced back through the internal jungle of the ship and found Wash looking around with wild eyes. He smelled like sweaty metal and she

realized it was the blood. It had soaked near half his less-than-tasteful shirt now. She dropped down next to him and whispered, "Be quiet."

"Kaylee —" he whispered back, "they're getting in. Go start the engine."

"It's not done."

"Will it start?"

"No."

"Are you sure?"

"I'm almost certain."

"Go and start the damn engine."

She shook her head. Then he started talking louder. And louder:

"Go. START IT. *GO*."

Now from outside there was a shout and there were running feet. So she had no choice. She swore at Wash over her shoulder as she ran.

She approached the main body of the engine. She was out of breath, shaking. She started the reactor. It made a sound not unlike Wash's wet cough. Then it died.

She reached past the shielding, thinking of Wash, feeling the awful hot-ants feeling on her skin. This was the deadly life's-blood of the ship. A definite no-touch-'em, but... she forced open a tiny stuck valve... The reactor coughed again and then her feet left the floor. So did a dozen dead rats and a few live ones, twisting and exclaiming.

She whipped her hand out of the engine. She had done it. They were floating. The grav rotor was negating the junkyard's gravity as it buoyed the ship.

The lack of gravity made her feel much worse. She'd already felt light-headed and making that literal was too much for her. The only thing that really helped was seeing Wash swimming toward her. If the lack of gravity had been bad for her, it had been very good for him. He was holding his left arm braced across his chest, but he was swimming with the right, brushing floating rats out of the way as he pushed off in the direction of the bridge.

A live rat did a fancy little swan dive into her line of sight. Kaylee shoved it away and watched Wash go.

Six hours later, Simon was assessing the amount of radiation she'd been exposed to. Across the room, Zoe was bent over Wash's cot, doing her best to embrace him without causing him pain. Kaylee tried to watch them, but Simon was being distracting on account of his existing.

"You'll be okay," he told her. She knew that's what he liked to say when he didn't have instruments good enough to tell him the truth.

"And Wash?"

"He'll be fine. I have everything I need to fix him."

Kaylee thought Zoe was probably everything he needed. Which brought the opposite question back to her mind again. Why was he what Zoe needed?

"I know why Zoe loves him," she told Simon, speaking softly, which made him lean in. Bonus.

He glanced over at them.

"Why?"

"He's a carrier."

"What? Like with a disease?"

"Yeah. Just like that."

"I don't understand."

Kaylee remembered their conversations between the decks of the Series One and she knew one of them had kept the other alive.

"He's a man what makes heroes."

THE WRITING PROCESS

By Jane Espenson

I've been asked to describe the writing process on a Joss Whedon show. I am primarily a *Buffy* writer, and I'm not in the *Firefly* writing room that often, but the general procedure is similar.

Okay, first there is the idea. This is usually something that Joss brings in, and it always begins with the main character – in my case, almost always with Buffy. We spend a lot of time discussing her emotional state, and how we want her to change over the course of the season. Frequently this in itself will suggest a story area – we will find a story in which we explore her mental state metaphorically. The episode 'Same Time, Same Place', was centered around Willow... we wanted to explore her emotional distance from the other characters. This turned into a story in which no one could see or touch Willow and vice versa. The episode 'Conversations with Dead People' dealt in part with Buffy's ambivalent feelings about her calling. She explored the feelings during a mock therapy session with a vampire she was destined to kill. Notice that the episode ideas *begin* with "what is she going through?" and never with "what would be a cool Slaying challenge?"

Once we have the central theme of the episode, and we understand how the main character will change during it, we begin "breaking" the story. This is done as a group, with the entire staff participating, except for anyone who is currently out writing the script for the previous week's episode. Breaking the story means organizing it into acts and scenes. When the break is complete, the white board in the writers' room is covered in blue marker, with a brief ordered description of each scene.

The first step in breaking an episode, once we know what the story is about, is deciding on the act breaks. These are the moments before each commercial that introduce danger or unexpected revelations into the story... the moments that make you come back after the commercials. Finding these moments in the story help give it shape: think of them as tentpoles that support the structure.

Selecting the moments that will be the act breaks is crucial. Writers who are just starting out, writing sample scripts that they will use to find that first job, often fail to realize this – I remember changing what the act break would be in a script because I wanted it to fall on the correct page. This is a bad sign. The act break moments

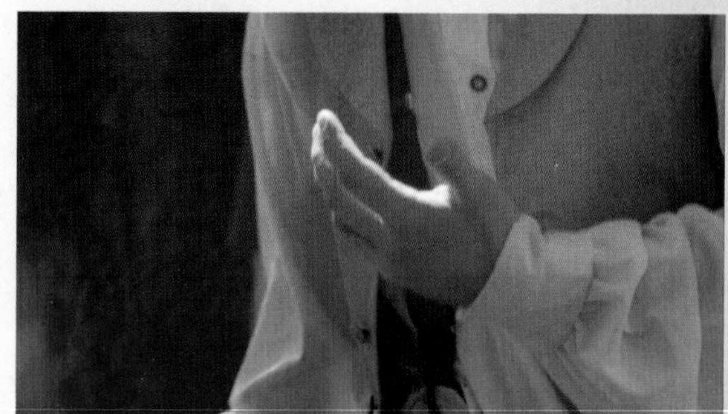

should be clear and large. In my *Firefly* episode, 'Shindig', the third act ends with Mal stabbed, badly injured, in danger of losing the duel. It does not end when Mal turns the fight around, when he stands victorious over his opponent. They're both big moments, but one of them leaves you curious and the other doesn't.

After the act breaks are set, the writers work together to fill in the surrounding scenes. When this is done, there is one white board full of material. At this point the work-dynamic changes completely, and it stops being a group project. At this point, the single author of the episode takes over. She takes the broken story and turns it into an outline. (Or possibly a "beat sheet", a less detailed version of an outline.) An outline is usually between nine and fourteen pages of typed material that fleshes out the broken story. It clarifies the attitudes of the characters, the order in which events happen within scenes, and often includes sample dialogue and jokes. A writer usually writes an outline in a single day.

The complete outline is turned in to the showrunners – Joss Whedon and Marti Noxon on *Buffy* or Joss and Tim Minear on *Firefly*. The writer is given notes on the outline very quickly, usually within the day. These notes are often quite brief and almost always have to do with the *tone* of the scenes – "make sure this doesn't get too silly," or "I see this as more genuinely scary."

At that point, the writer starts work, writing the script itself. Many of the writers go home to do this. They are excused from story breaking until their first draft is done. (The rest of the staff, of course, moves on to breaking the next episode.) The writing of a first draft takes anywhere from three days to two weeks, depending on the demands of production. Sometimes the production schedule requires that more than one writer work on a given episode, splitting it into halves or even thirds – interestingly, this often results in very nice episodes and isn't as jarring as you might expect, because we've all learned to write in the same style.

The first draft turns a dozen-page outline into approximately 52 pages of action and dialogue. People outside the writing process are sometimes disappointed to learn that we are following a detailed outline. They feel that there can be little creative work left to do in the actual writing, but this is not the case. This is, in fact, the most exciting and freeing part of the process... every word spoken, every punch thrown, is spelled out by the writer at this stage. For me, this, more than during filming, is when the episode actually becomes *real*.

After the first draft is turned in, the writer gets another set of notes. These may be light or extensive, but on a Joss Whedon show, these rarely result in a rethinking of the episode. The broken story remains the same, although the words expressing it may change. Even an extensive note session rarely lasts more than an hour, and usually is much shorter than that. The writer takes these notes and in the next few days, produces a second draft. *Buffy* scripts usually go to a third draft and sometimes a fourth, but by the end of the process the changes become very small indeed – "change this word" or "cut this joke."

At the end of the process, Joss or Marti or Tim usually take the script and make a quick rewriting pass of their own. This produces the SHOOTING DRAFT.

Then it is filmed!

Congratulations – that's an episode!

ORIGINALLY PUBLISHED ON FOX.COM, 2002

NATHAN FILLION

Captain Malcolm Reynolds

NATHAN ON THE LONGEVITY OF THE FANBASE:
When I was doing *Firefly*, I thought the show would last a long time. That it didn't was a surprise to me, and then likewise, for such a short life, that it's had such incredible legs, that has been a surprise. I knew it would live in my heart, because I really enjoyed it, I had a great time, and I can't deny that I learned so much from that project, I learned so much from Joss, but no, I had no idea [the fandom would last so long]. Pleasantly surprised!

INTERVIEW WITH ABBIE BERNSTEIN, 2009

ON WHY HE LOVES THE FANS:
There's nothing like going to Edinburgh, a place where I've never been – it's a whole other country – and you come in and there's a theatre full of 800 people who are right there, hanging on your every word, and laughing at all my crappy jokes.

INTERVIEW WITH CHUCK THE MOVIE GUY, 2005

ON STARTING OUT HIS CAREER IN THE SOAP *ONE LIFE TO LIVE*:
Bob Woods, he played my uncle, he played Bo Buchanan. I was Joey Buchanan, and two years into my three-year contract he pulled me aside and said, "Look, I'm here to tell you that they are going to come and renegotiate your contract. I'm telling you, say no. The harder you say no, the harder they are going to make it to leave. They offer you more money, but daytime drama is the golden handcuffs; they're gold, but they're handcuffs. If you leave and go to LA and try it out, if it doesn't work out they'll take you back, so go out there and try your luck." So every time I go to New York, I buy Bob a bottle of something nice.

INTERVIEW WITH ZETAMINOR.COM, 2005

NATHAN FILLION

ON A SOURCE OF INSPIRATION FOR HIS PERFORMANCE AS MAL:
A friend of mine grew up in Texas and he worked on a farm with his grandfather. He would tell me these amazing stories of his grandfather, who can't be flustered. This one story that particularly struck me was, they were castrating bulls. The process is that you throw them into this stall, close the gate behind them, do your business and get the next one in there. While they're getting this one bull in, they're shutting the gate, the bull kicked and hit the gate between his thumb and a post. And it severed his thumb, which remained inside his glove, but it was hanging. He was, "Oh well, we have six more to do, so let's keep this going." He didn't show the pain in any way. And there's my friend Cory, nine, ten years old going, "Grandpa, you have to go to the hospital!" crying. Because of him he decided to go, but I think he was a tough man. He's had some hard living. That's the kind of man I imagined Malcolm to be, he grew up on a ranch. He's a hard worker, not somebody who cries from a little pain.

INTERVIEW WITH ZETAMINOR.COM, 2005

ON HIS 'FIGHT CLUB' TRAINING REGIME FOR THE MOVIE, COMPARED TO SUMMER GLAU'S:
I was there barely three weeks. And I would complain about my time there, and every time I'd come in, I'd see

Summer doing her thing, kicking something above her head about sixty times. I'd be warming up and doing my stuff, cool down and leave, and she's in the corner fighting nine guys. And she had to start months before us. She worked really hard.

INTERVIEW WITH ZETAMINOR.COM, 2005

JEWEL STAITE AND MORENA BACCARIN ON NATHAN BEING THE 'LEADER' OF THE CAST, BOTH ONSCREEN AND OFF:

Jewel: I think we all naturally follow Nathan without realizing that we are following Nathan. We were all on set one day and sitting in our chairs on a break and somebody walked by with a platter of sandwiches to take to the craft services table. Nathan said, "Oh hey they've got sandwiches, let's go check it out." And everybody went [mimes standing up and following after Nathan], and then we kind of looked at each other and said, "Why are we following him? We just ate. I'm not even hungry!" I just do as he tells me.

Morena: It's true, we all kind of just follow the Captain. It's written in there, we may as well do it! But no joke, I'm going to take a serious note here – I'm not kidding. When I first came to the set everybody was already there, and I found the tone had been set for what we were to expect from each other and the work, and I attribute a lot of that to Nathan. I felt like we were a family and I would be taken care of – there were several incidences during the shoot in which I came to Nathan for help with certain things and he was right there. I feel like that's 100 percent the case.

SPEAKING ON STAGE AT THE 'SERENITY' CONVENTION, 2005

ON 'OUT OF GAS':

I really enjoy that moment of seeing Malcolm Reynolds looking across that ship yard and seeing Serenity lying up there in the blowing sand. I think that's the moment where he fell in love. Joss Whedon said it was like seeing a girl across a dance floor and falling for them – love at first sight.

SPEAKING ON STAGE AT 'THE WHITE ROOM' CONVENTION, 2004

ON WHY *FIREFLY* IS PARTICULARLY SPECIAL TO HIM:

I've had jobs that I've preferred more than others simply because I've gotten to meet and make friends with great people. I've pulled at least one very close friend from every project I've done with the exception of *Firefly*, where I pulled all of them – they're *all* my friends.

INTERVIEW WITH FIRSTSHOWING.NET, 2007

BATTLE PLANS

Storyboarding the Battle of Serenity Valley

"I got involved with *Firefly* in the very beginning stages," remembers Charles Ratteray, a Los Angeles-based storyboard artist, concept designer and illustrator, who started out as a special effects intern at Stan Winston Studio thirteen years ago, and has since worked as a freelancer on such memorable TV shows as *Battlestar Galactica*, *Buffy the Vampire Slayer* and *CSI*.

It was Ratteray's job to help turn the Battle of Serenity Valley from the 'EXT. SERENITY VALLEY – NIGHT: Battle rages' of Joss Whedon's script into the tense, attention-grabbing sequence that was originally planned to launch the entire series.

"Loni Peristere of Zoic Studios came to me and asked me to board out the first battle sequence in episode one," Ratteray continues. "He was my main window into the production part of the *Firefly* experience. When necessary I accompanied him into meetings with Joss and the rest of the creative crew over there. For the most part I completed the boards at Zoic and at my private studio."

Though the artist also contributed some ship designs, and storyboarded other sequences for the series (some of which are featured in the 'Ships of the 'Verse' section

of this book), that opening scene remains his favorite: "It really set the mood, and had loads of action and emotion driving the visuals. And of course it was a kick-ass way to set the tone of the episode."

All these years later, as he dug deep into his archive to supply the art that is published here for the first time, he still has fond memories of his time on the series. "*Firefly* was an awesome show. Masterfully thought out and thoroughly entertaining. It's not surprising it has generated such a loyal following. As far as the Browncoats go, they're really, really cool. 'Keep the torch burning, never give up' – I can definitely identify with that line of thinking."

❖ This spread and overleaf: Ratteray's storyboards for the sequence contain some shots that were ultimately not filmed.

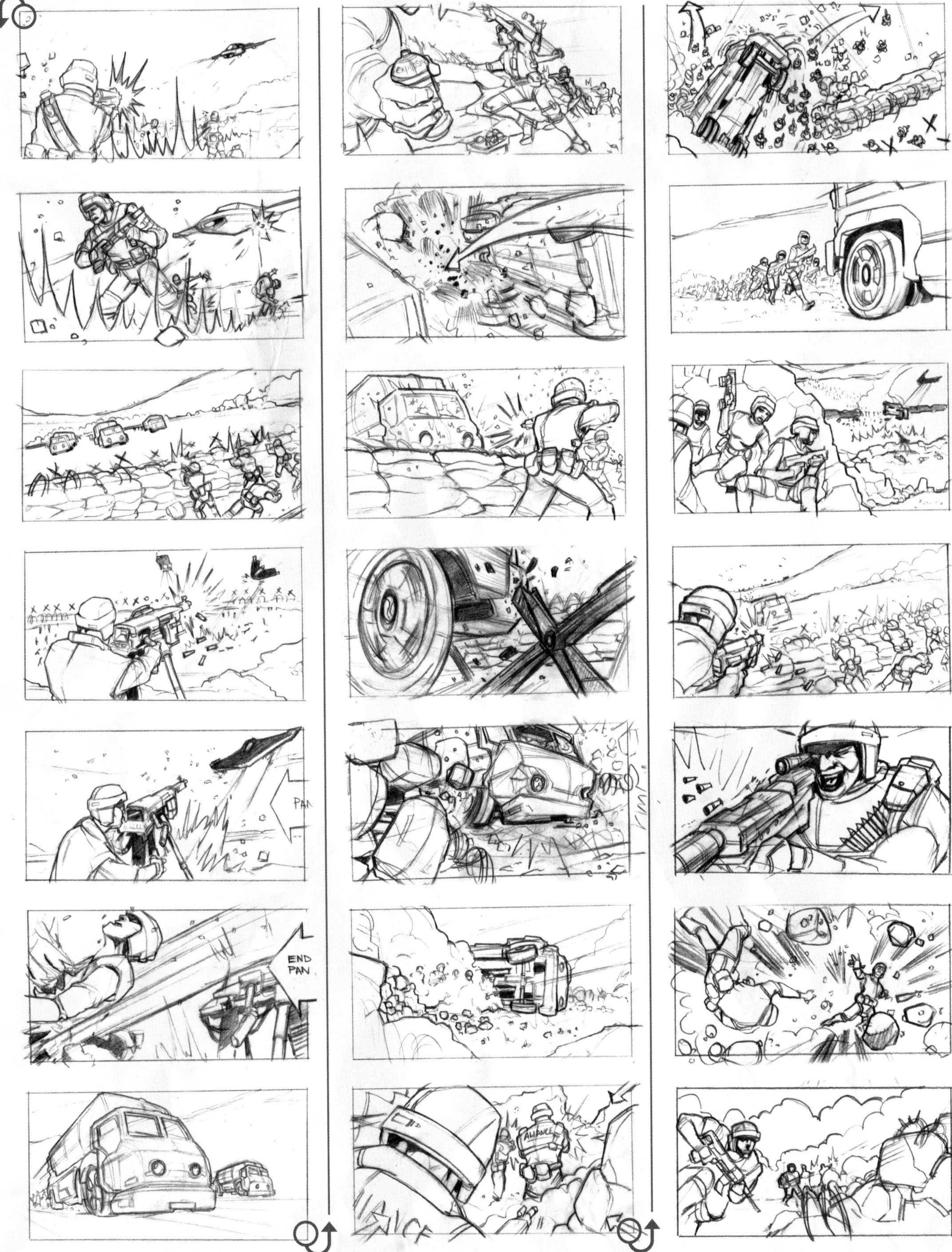
PAN
END PAN

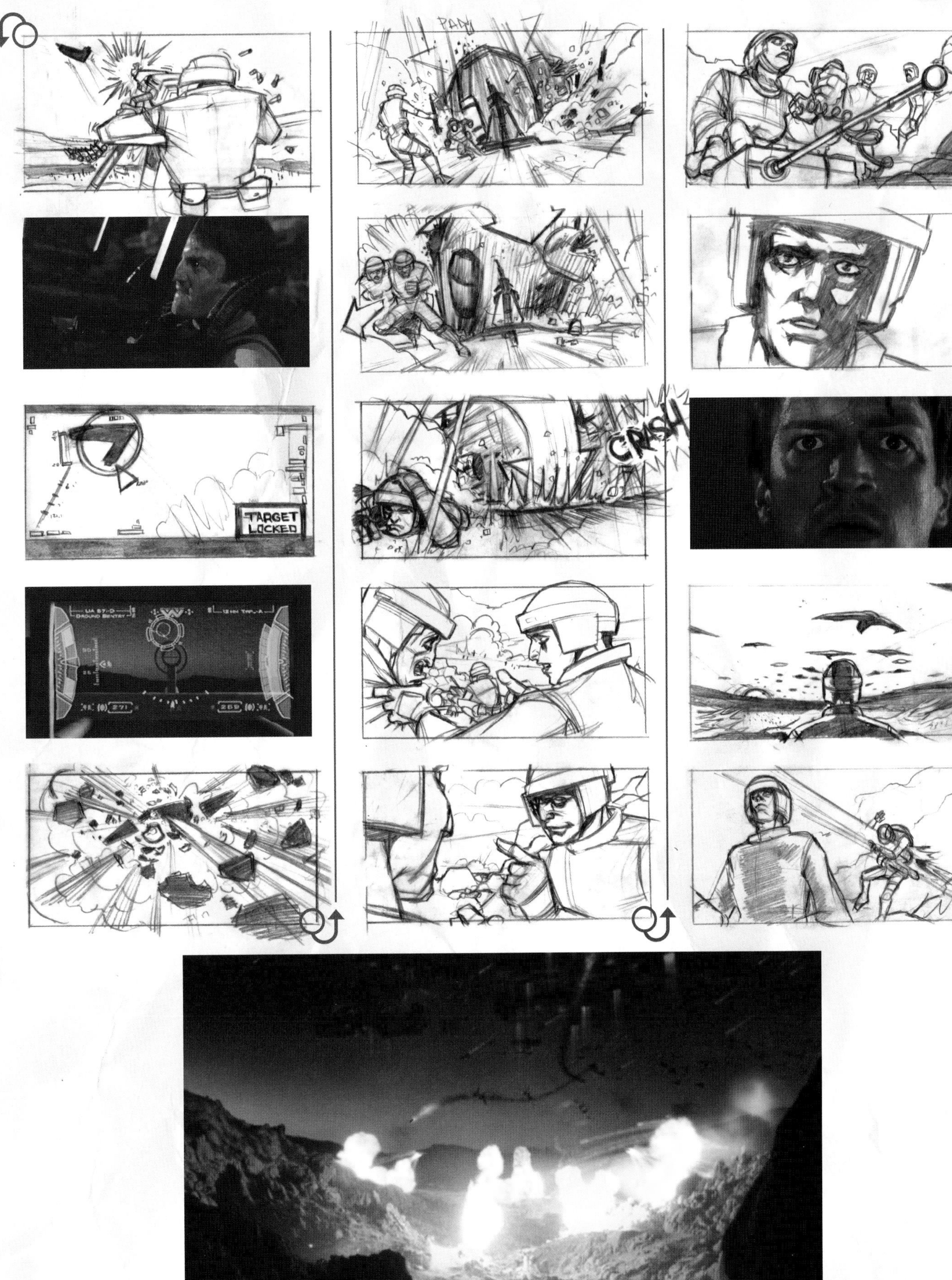
PAP
CRASH
TARGET LOCKED

GINA TORRES

Zoe Washburne

GINA ON WHY JOSS CAST HER AS ZOE:
I think he hired me because he saw a great deal of what he had written and so there was never really a whole lot of discussion. He felt confident and comfortable with what I was bringing to the table, which is a quiet authority. Zoe's presence is more often more important than anything that she can say. When she speaks, it's always for a reason; for a particular reason. She's not talking just to be talking. I think that if Zoe is displeased or if she's happy, we want to feel like the temperature is literally changing in the room, and that was my job.

INTERVIEW WITH BLACKFILM.COM, 2005

ON THE PROMINENT ROLES FOR WOMEN IN THE 'VERSE:
I was happy about it. Clearly when you are looking into the future... as far as we've come now, you have women in the trenches now, they are in Iraq and in the work place. If you project that 500 years into the future, of course we are going to be in positions of power and be even more capable, because we are part of the workforce. As human beings we have to use each other and what we're best at. And my character Zoe is clearly a fabulous, kick-ass, capable soldier. Why wouldn't you want that person to be your right hand?

INTERVIEW WITH ZETAMINOR.COM, 2005

ON THE SHOW'S DISTINCTIVE DIALOGUE:
What is so interesting about the writing, is that [Joss] has taken this futuristic world that he has created and all the circumstances that have sort of fed into this world that you see in front of you, and an element of that is what we refer to as 'Joss speak'. It's the English language ever so tweaked enough to make you a little crazy [laughs] as an actor, but it sort of informs everything else surrounding it, so maybe a line that you may have heard before doesn't sound the same. Because it doesn't sound the same it holds a different weight, or it resonates differently in the ears, and I think that just makes it more interesting.

INTERVIEW WITH ZETAMINOR.COM, 2005

GINA TORRES

ON THE FANS' REACTION TO THE CANCELLATION:

Some were angry [laughs], most of them were sad. They found us early, they were sort of shocked that we disappeared because we were on the air for eleven episodes and we were pre-empted as often as we aired. We might be on one week and then we wouldn't be on for two weeks because of the baseball playoffs or whatever it was. They felt like they were teased with the promise of a show that they could be dedicated to and be interested in and see how it played out. And then we were gone as quickly as we appeared. I think that's what helped with the sales of the DVD, suddenly there was enough talk about it, maybe enough people had seen it, but they were just completely dissatisfied and wanted to know what happened. Because it is good storytelling, they are intriguing characters, and, you know, how do you feel when your favorite show is cancelled? You feel lost a little bit. *Cheers* was on the air for years and people still miss that show! I think we just sort of filled a niche that wasn't available on television at the time.

But it is incredibly gratifying to be a part of something that you knew was special from the very beginning, that was not understood. There was really no effort, that we could see, to make that happen and then it [was] released to the world and the world responded in the way that it has... yes, absolutely it's incredibly vindicating.

INTERVIEW WITH ZETAMINOR.COM, 2005

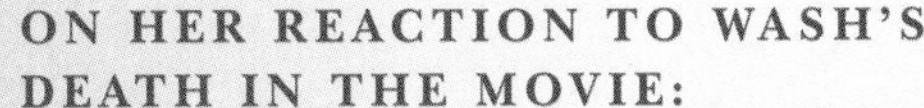

ON HER REACTION TO WASH'S DEATH IN THE MOVIE:

There was definitely a collective gasp heard across the nation when we all got the script and read it. I adored Alan, and I adored him as Wash, as my pretend husband. I thought we were an amazing couple. In a way, it might hurt you to hear this, but since there is no sequel to *Serenity* it is a relief, because I can't imagine Zoe without him. I really can't.

INTERVIEW WITH IFMAGAZINE.COM, 2006

OBJECTS IN SPACE

Props

A selection of Firefly props

Some of the props in this section have become iconic amongst the Browncoats, while others were only glimpsed onscreen. All of them, however, played their part in adding to the rich texture of the 'verse...

ALLIANCE SONIC RIFLE

EPISODES: 'TRASH' AND 'ARIEL'

This is an unusual prop. It's a rare example of a non-lethal weapon in science fiction. It's in good company: the phaser from the original *Star Trek* had a stun setting.

The design is a deliberate choice by Joss Whedon and the producers to allow the possibility of an essentially harmless weapon in the 'verse. The theory is simple: compressed and focused sound waves in a narrow frequency band.

Originally one of eight made by Applied Effects in Los Angeles, this prop appeared twice in *Firefly*, both times in the hands of purplebellies. At the time of printing of the first *Official Companion* books, the whereabouts of the screen-used props was unknown. One has since come to light.

This prop is also unusual in that there was not time to make rubber stunt copies of it, so the Sonics used in the fight and action sequences are fully detailed 'hero' versions. The four surviving Sonics do show evidence of a tough life.

It is a heavy, solid piece, made in five resin sections cemented together. The emitter tip is of machined aluminum with red painted details. The models for the emitter focus dishes were modified *Flintstones* jello dishes. The color scheme is a dark metallic blue with gunmetal and silver details.

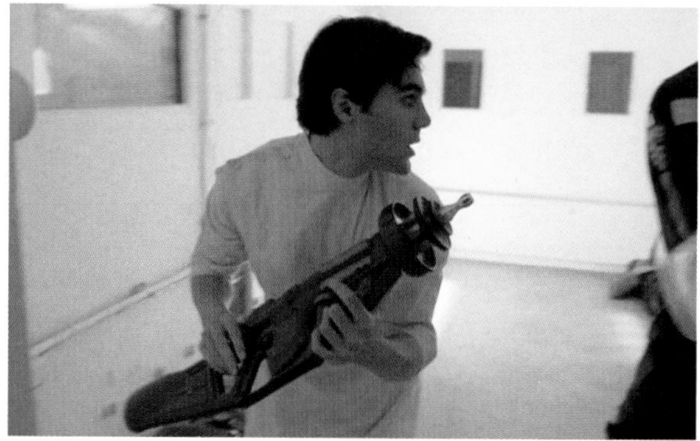

There's an interesting 'technical' section on each side, apparently made from bashed model kit parts.

The base prop for the original model was a 'Foosh' rifle from the Arnold Schwarzenegger film *The Sixth Day*, also made by Applied Effects.

Not bad for "high-tech Alliance crap".

BOOK'S BIBLE

MULTIPLE EPISODES

At a mere 6 inches by 4.25 inches by 1.25 inches, this King James compact reference version of the Holy Bible, from Thomas Nelson publishers, doesn't look like anything special, other than being the 'Good Book' of course.

This leather-clad tome, now bearing the signature of one Ron Glass, appears in the opening sequence of *Firefly* and is the badge of office of Shepherd Derrial Book.

The script for the episode 'Jaynestown' required River to mutilate Book's Bible in an attempt to 'fix' it. Summer Glau insisted on undertaking the task herself. The prop is annotated throughout with blue, red, green and orange marker; some of the pages are folded and some torn out altogether.

On page 108, "Jesus loves me this I know" is written in blue pen.

The Bible was sourced by the on-set propmaster Skip Crank, and was one of several shown to Joss Whedon as likely candidates for the Shepherd's constant companion. Gifted to Ron Glass when the show was cancelled, the Bible remained in Ron's care until it was auctioned for charity at the Flanvention in December 2005. Ron signed the book for the lucky winner.

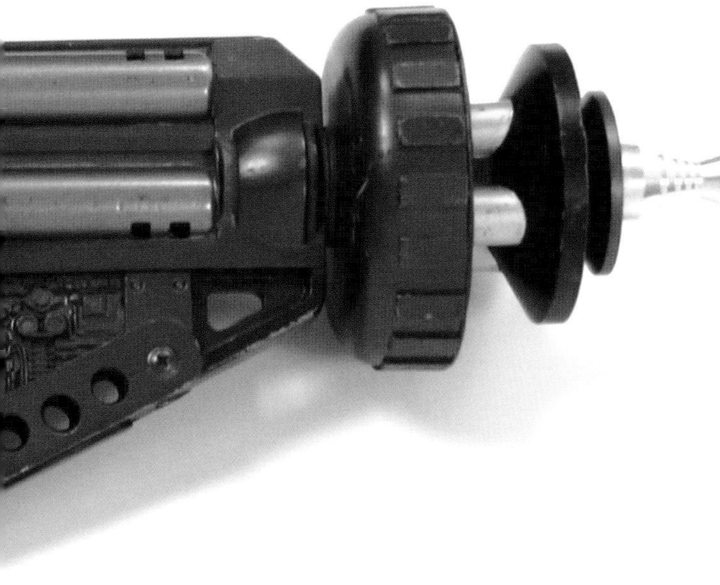

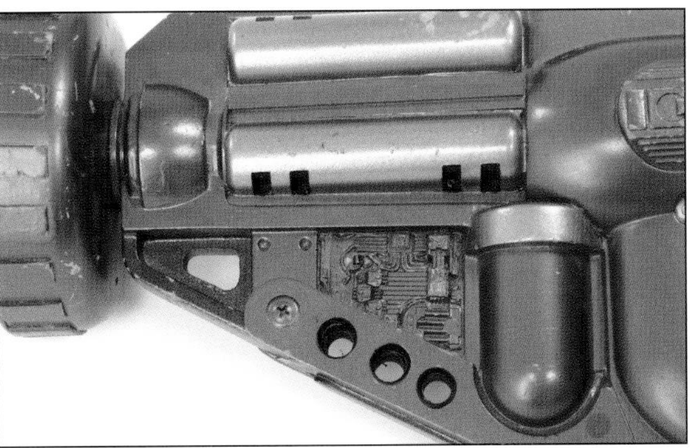

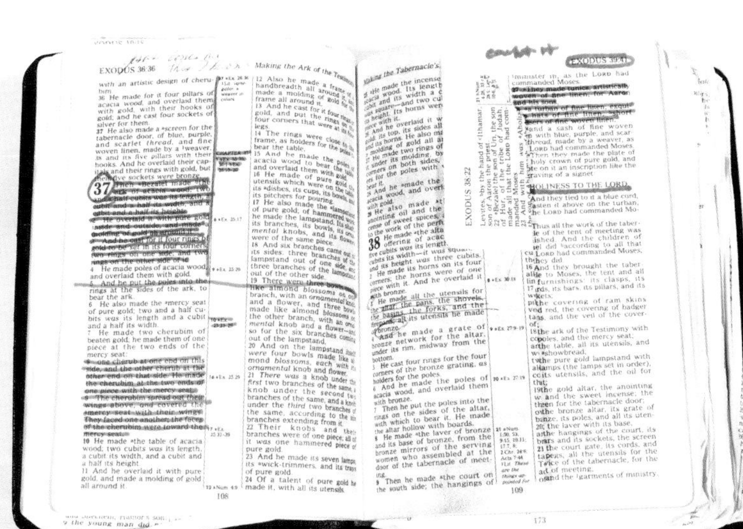

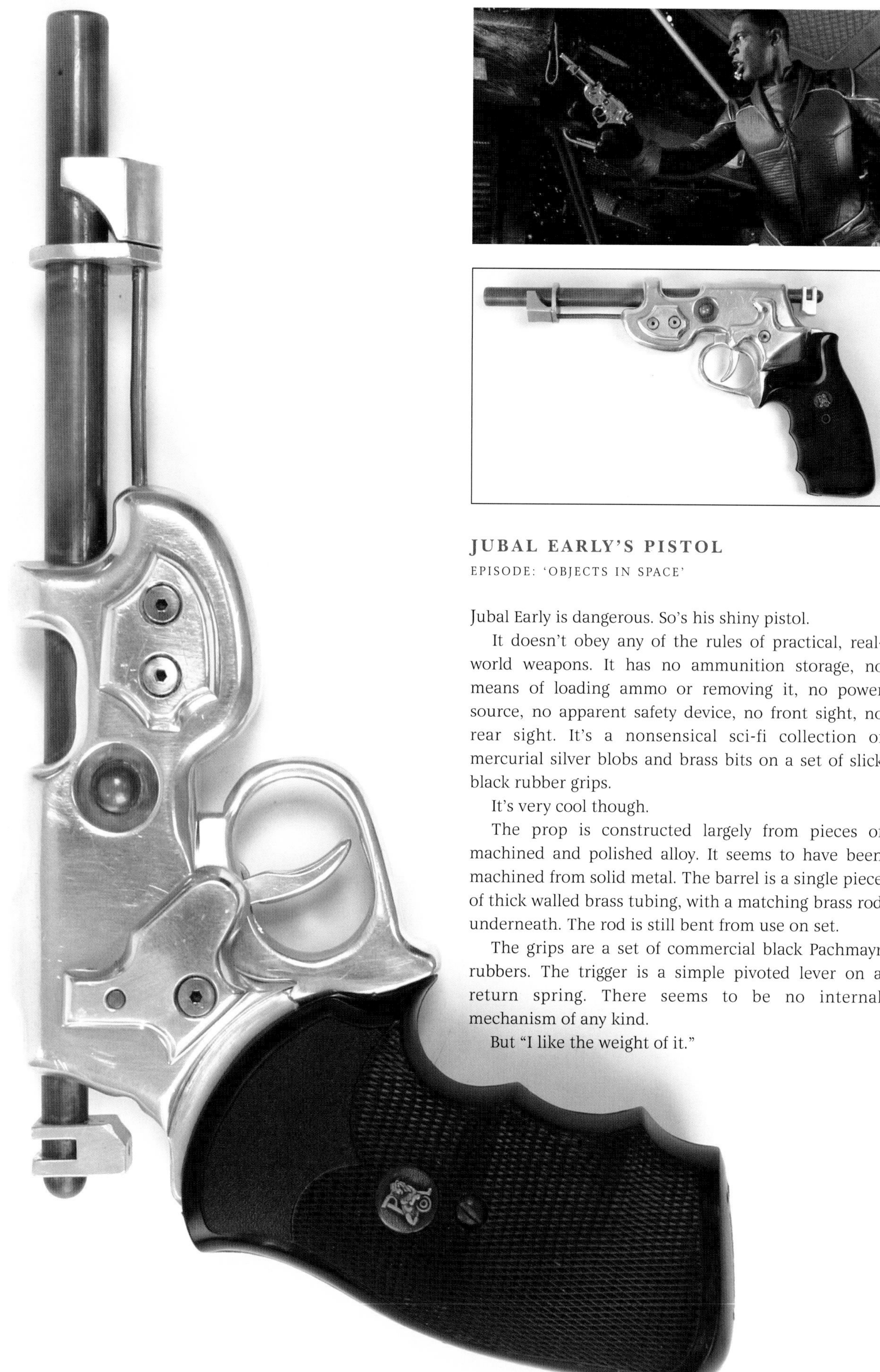

JUBAL EARLY'S PISTOL

EPISODE: 'OBJECTS IN SPACE'

Jubal Early is dangerous. So's his shiny pistol.

It doesn't obey any of the rules of practical, real-world weapons. It has no ammunition storage, no means of loading ammo or removing it, no power source, no apparent safety device, no front sight, no rear sight. It's a nonsensical sci-fi collection of mercurial silver blobs and brass bits on a set of slick black rubber grips.

It's very cool though.

The prop is constructed largely from pieces of machined and polished alloy. It seems to have been machined from solid metal. The barrel is a single piece of thick walled brass tubing, with a matching brass rod underneath. The rod is still bent from use on set.

The grips are a set of commercial black Pachmayr rubbers. The trigger is a simple pivoted lever on a return spring. There seems to be no internal mechanism of any kind.

But "I like the weight of it."

BURGESS' LASER

EPISODE: 'HEART OF GOLD'

Few bad guys are as bad as Rance Burgess, the archetypal evil-local-landowner-who's-brought-a-town-to-its-knees. Burgess is self-appointed judge, jury and executioner who makes his own "distinction between legality and morality".

'Heart of Gold' is a very traditional story of good versus evil. Folks in distress (usually some kind of dress, anyway), rescued by hired guns from out of town — its theme is repeated throughout the history of film and television. Clint Eastwood's *Unforgiven* is a good modern example.

So — Burgess is a bad man. It's only fitting that such a villain has an appropriately evil weapon: a Silk-Trigger, Active Return-Bolt Laser, with the Auto Target-Adjust "crafted special".

This is quite an unexpected sight. Weirdly for *Firefly*, it's actually a bona fide Sci-Fi Raygun. The best, and flashiest, that money can buy. Does he have a horse, like his men?

No, he has a silver hovercraft...

Joss Whedon leads us once again down the garden

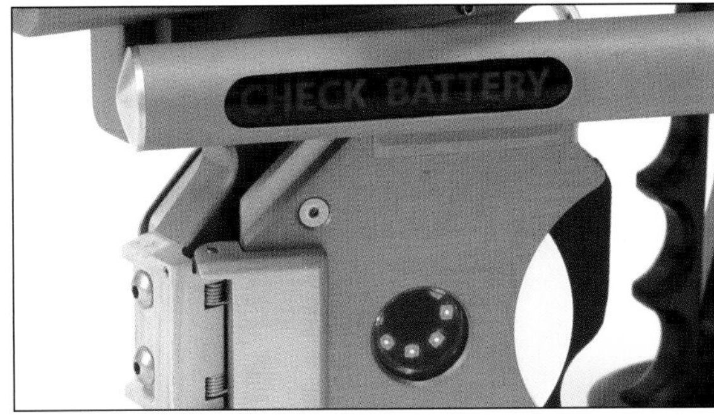

path of blindly trusting technology. Burgess puts his misplaced trust in the Laser and is, naturally, let down at the crucial moment by a flat battery.

The prop itself is extremely well made. It seems to have been machined from solid alloy billets — a tremendous amount of work. It has a lot of very cool light functions, including two rows of red running lights on the top, red firing 'lasers' in the twin barrels and a circular chase circuit in the side window that changes colors when you open the side panel.

And then there's the oversized 'Check Battery' warning. Hilarious.

Yep, "She is a beauty."

EMERGENCY BREATHING MASKS

MULTIPLE EPISODES

The 'verse can be a dangerous place. It pays to have certain safeguards to hand should the worst-case scenario materialize.

Serenity's interior sets were designed to reflect the difficulties faced by her crew in an imperfect world. Every part of the ship's design shows an awareness of the potential issues of the environment. Nowhere is this more clearly seen than at the hatchways in the ship's bulkheads.

In sea-going vessels on Earth, watertight doors were placed in bulkheads strategically positioned to enable areas of the ship to be sealed off, should they become damaged. This would prevent the flooding of additional compartments if the vessel became holed.

Designers of ships intended for use in space would face a similar issue should a meteorite strike or weapons fire breach the hull of their ship. The air in the damaged compartment would be vented to space. Sure, you wouldn't drown, but the upshot is the same; bloated and blue, curled in the fetal position. Far from ideal, you'll agree.

Serenity has airtight bulkheads between each major section of the ship, and at either side of each door is an emergency breathing mask. Thoughtfully located for your safety and convenience, should you end up on the wrong side of a door.

The sixteen masks used on the set are obsolete high-altitude emergency masks, used to deliver oxygen to military aircrews.

The masks are primarily rubber and retro white and grey plastic, but have exciting anodized aluminum parts and hoses and a push-to-talk microphone button. The little audio connectors on the end of the cable were added by the Art Department, so they could plug into the bulkhead on the set.

Though if you were to be trapped in a compartment with no air, it might be better to have a little air cylinder with your mask. That way, you could move more than five feet away from the door...

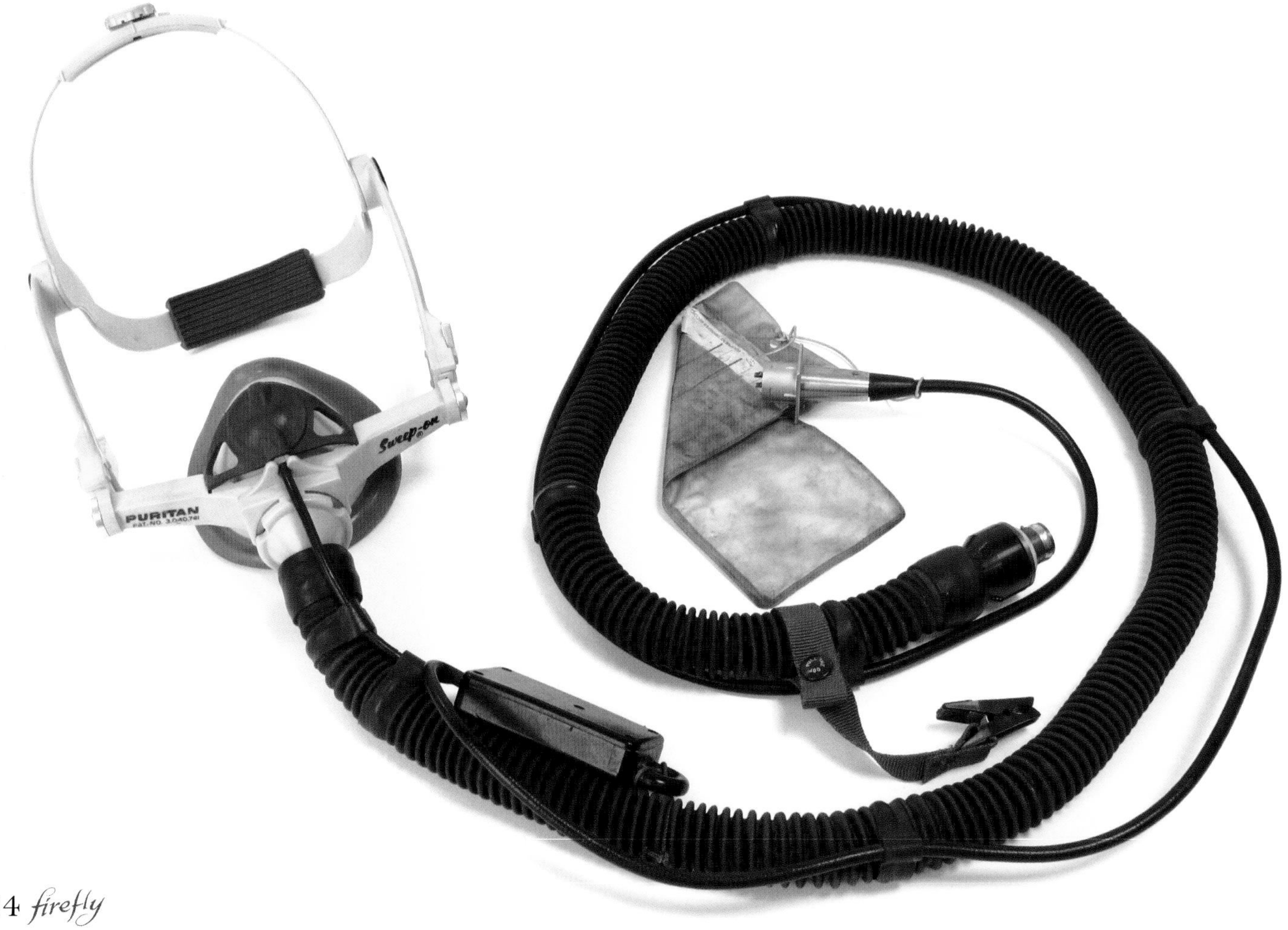

GALLEY WARE

MULTIPLE EPISODES

The galley is the heart of the ship. Bad things as well as good can happen to a heart, and Serenity's galley has seen the best of times and the worst of times for our intrepid crew. Birthdays, arguments, conflict, love and war.

The set was designed to be a little part of home in space. It's a warm, inviting space and the huge table brings Thanksgiving and Christmas family gatherings to mind. You can almost see Kaylee stenciling the flowers on the bulkheads.

Essential dressing for any galley set are the tools of the trade: pots, pans, knives and spoons.

The set was dressed by the *Firefly* Art Department, using items from prop rental houses in the Los Angeles area. Many of these rental houses have 'themed' sections, such as Medical or Police equipment. These props would be from the Restaurant section.

The chopsticks used in the mess are typical *Firefly*: a motley crew of mix-and-match items from many different cultures. Some are expensive Core Planet lacquer-ware, others the basic wooden sticks of a farmer out on the Rim.

The orange/brown, oriental serving containers appear in virtually every episode, as do the big pans and spoons hanging on the rack.

The two aluminum dredgers are standard kitchen equipment, used in *Firefly* as salt shakers. One has a bent handle, damaged when Zoe was blown up in 'Out of Gas'.

In many ways the galley is the most important set in the show. For many of the cast and crew, the happiest times on *Firefly* were in the mess hall, gathered around the table laughing.

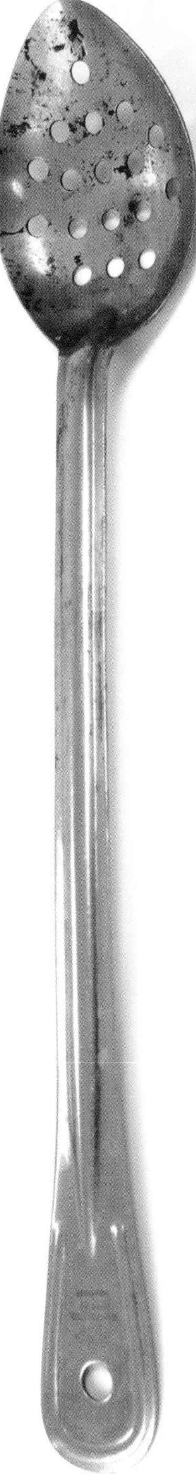

JAYNE'S FLYING GEAR

EPISODES: 'THE TRAIN JOB', 'JAYNESTOWN'

Never averse to taking a risk, Jayne is seen hanging out the bottom of a spaceship more than once.

Back in the real world, the prospect of one of your lead actors dangling in space above a stage floor is a pretty daunting one for any producer. This kind of activity is usually reserved for stunt performers. Adam Baldwin is an intrepid type though, and you can clearly see it's Adam himself in many of the fight sequences and stunts throughout the series.

This is actually a custom-made flying harness, used by stunt performers in film and television. It's constructed of very sturdy nylon strapping and has a safe 'lifting point' on the back of the shoulders. There are leg loops, like a parachute harness, to help keep the wearer's body in a stable attitude and to help spread the load of their bodyweight around.

The goggles are standard issue US Military eyewear, now obsolete. They have a soft foam face seal, which on the pair used in 'Jaynestown' was cut away to show Adam's face more clearly.

JAYNE'S KNIFE

EPISODE: 'JAYNESTOWN'

In 'Jaynestown', we get a little glimpse into the past of our enigmatic mercenary. Here's a look at a key prop from the episode: Jayne's 'other' knife.

The knife is actually a whole set of props, comprising four versions for different purposes.

The first is the detailed 'hero' version. This is a heavy, solid metal knife, used in close up shots. The antler hilt is a resin casting of a real deer antler, and the brass ferrule is exactly what it appears to be. Although made from steel, the blade is 'safe', with no live, sharpened edge.

There is also a rubber, 'stunt' version of the knife, less detailed than the hero. This is a prop used in medium or long shots, whenever the actor is moving in an action sequence, and could possibly hurt himself with it. You can spot the stunt version in Adam Baldwin's hand when he pushes the statue over.

The third version seen here is a 'plate' knife. It is made of steel, but is only half a knife. The flat, steel end of the blade is drilled and tapped and can be screwed to a flat metal plate worn under the actor's clothing. This same trick was used for Mal, when stabbed by Crow in 'The Train Job'.

There is a fourth version, not pictured — a retractable knife. This has one section of the blade which telescopes into another, to give the illusion of the knife stabbing someone. Such props tend to work better when being 'pulled out' of the stab victim.

We can only guess at why the producers decided to give Jayne a different knife for this episode. One suspects there was no plate or retractable version of Jayne's regular knife, and no time or budget to have them made.

A memorable prop, from "the man they call Jayne".

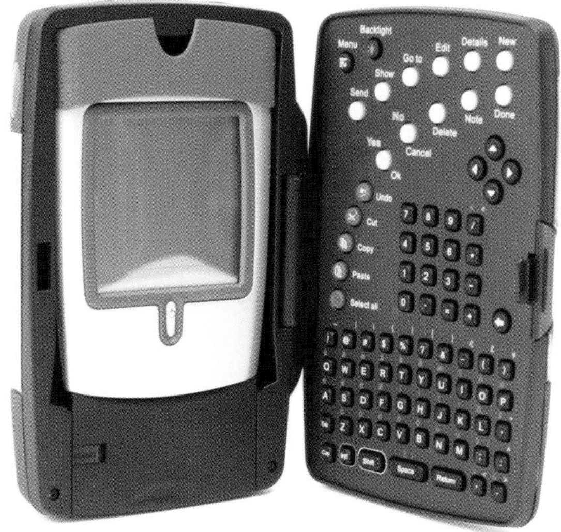

DOBSON'S CORTEX ACCESS DEVICE

EPISODE: 'SERENITY'

Shot in the face? Well, he had it coming...

Laurence Dobson, Alliance agent, hot on the trail of Simon and River Tam is hiding out aboard the independent freighter, Serenity.

An essential piece of equipment for the Alliance-mole-in-hiding is the Personal Cortex Access Device.

The concept is similar to that of an Earth-That-Was PDA or notebook computer. A compact, hand-held device capable of connecting the user to the 'verse's equivalent of the Internet, The Cortex.

Although perfect for purpose as a sci-fi device, the actual prop comprises two found items, real-world personal organizers, both now obsolete.

The two items were made by two separate companies and are in no way related, but the propmaster has managed to fuse them into a utilitarian-looking single unit.

The prop is constructed entirely from injection-molded plastics, the outer shell painted silver. The screen is not functional and never was — the active Cortex screen seen in the show was added in post-production.

The original operating stylus is missing, but other than that, it's in pretty good condition. Especially since it was thrown across the cabin by the frustrated Dobson!

The diligence of *Firefly* fans from all over the world, all wanting their own Cortex Device for costuming, has now made these two objects — the Franklin RF 8110 Rolodex and the Fellowes Type 'N' Go PDA/Organiser — very hard to find!

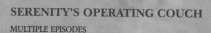

SERENITY'S OPERATING COUCH

MULTIPLE EPISODES

This chair is quite unusual.

It's an examination table, dentist's chair, operating table, psychiatrist's couch, pathologist's bench, field hospital, restraint device, morgue slab ... it even has stirrups for birthing, should the need arise.

This is, of course, the operating table from Serenity's infirmary set.

Somewhat unusually for a permanent dressing prop on a major television show, the chair was a rental from a large Hollywood prop house.

It was made by a company called Ritter, who still make medical examination tables. It is quite old, possibly 1940s or 50s, and weighs an incredible 300 pounds.

To the eye, it's a great deal less red than it appeared in *Firefly*, more russet or brown. Its silky smooth, precision engineered, positional locking system still operates perfectly, and its padded sections can be locked in any position. A substantial, solid piece of equipment.

Kaylee lay here shot and bleeding, Zoe was carried here injured, Jayne's 'Pine' was pronounced OK, Simon himself had Early's bullet extracted on it, River was sedated, a Reaver restrained, Book almost died here.

Mal injected himself in the heart with adrenalin here when he was Serenity's last hope.

It's seen a lot of action.

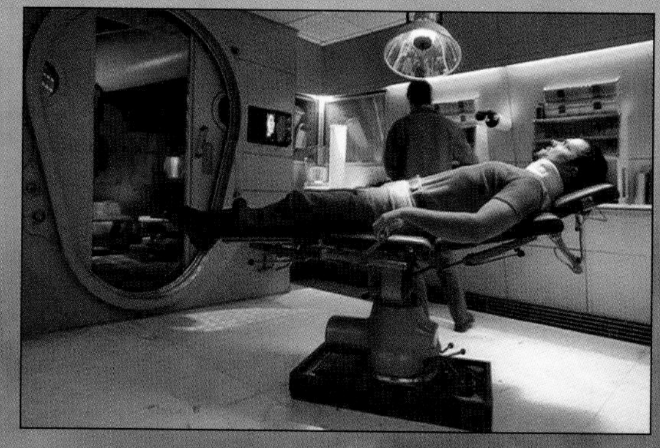

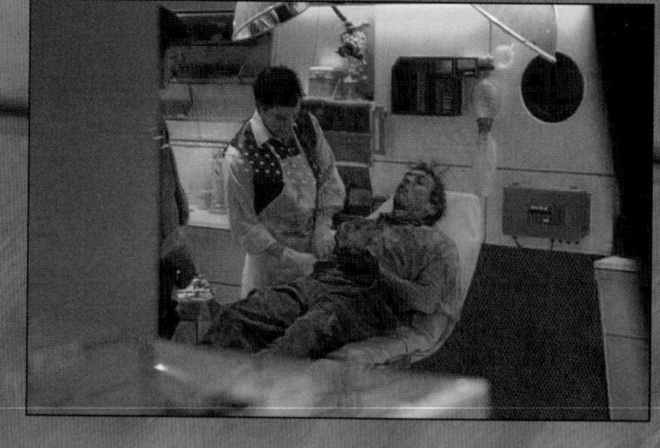

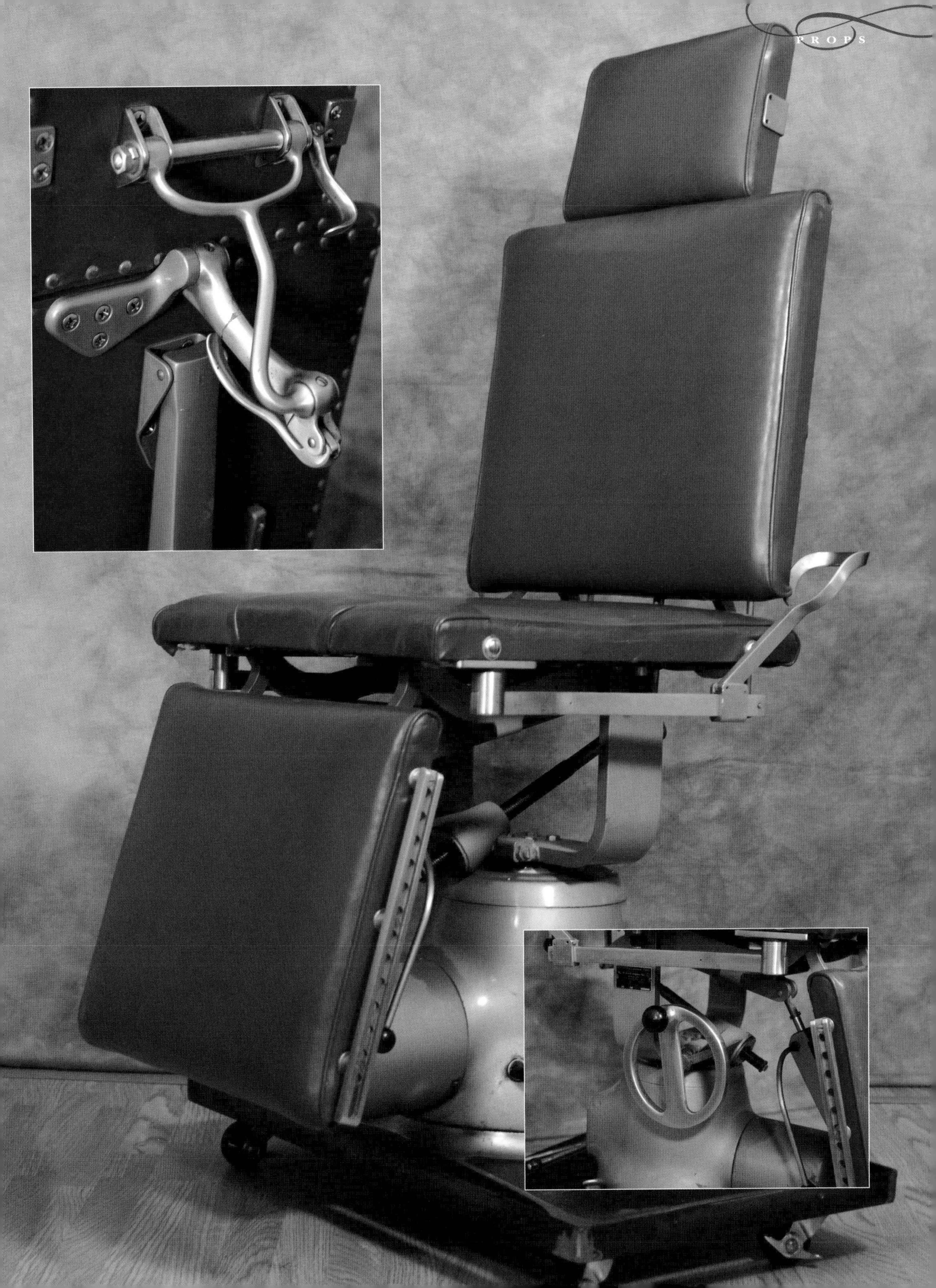

THE LASSITER

EPISODE: 'TRASH'

In *Firefly* the Lassiter is an historic relic, the first practical Laser weapon from Earth-That-Was. It's also a priceless antique, worthy of a traditional heist caper. This is not a new prop created for the show, but rather one that has served in Hollywood productions for many decades. It is known to have been in the inventory of a prominent prop rental house in Los Angeles as far back as 1992.

Firefly simply didn't have the budget to have every special prop custom made. Instead, the propmaster would go to rental houses and bring back samples of different styled weapons for the director to choose from. This is how the Lassiter was selected for *Firefly*. The prop is named for John Lasseter, a friend and collaborator of Joss Whedon, and Oscar-winning animator and director.

The Lassiter is never seen working in 'Trash', but the prop has several functions. The large display screen on the rear has several working lights and there is a functional red LED under each of the buttons at the side. There is also a descending numerical countdown on the top right of the screen. There is a red 'laser' light in the machined sight/probe on the top, and two transparent probes on the front end also light up.

Made largely from cast and machined metal, the prop has some weight to it — Morena Baccarin did very well to hold it at arm's length for any time in 'Trash'. It was smeared with some of the mud make-up from 'Jaynestown' to give it a weathered look for the episode, then wiped clean after use.

The main body of the prop is an old, converted rechargeable flashlight: the First Alert ReadyLite (below left). This would suggest the prop was made some time in the Eighties. The silver handle seems to be a solid aluminum foundry casting of a Sixties plastic toy ray gun called a 'Galactronic Gun' (below).

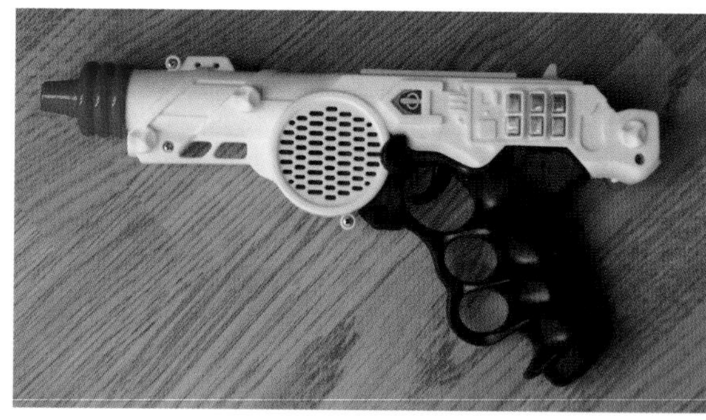

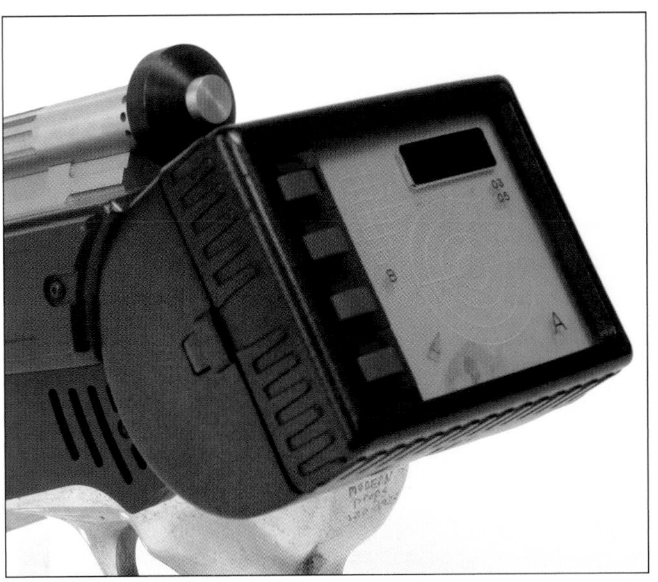
B
A

WASH'S DINOSAURS

MULTIPLE EPISODES

Wash never looks more at home than when in Serenity's cockpit, surrounded by his plastic pals.

Like the rest of the ship's crew, Wash's Dinos are an eclectic bunch. Their number includes models of all different colors, sizes and scales and seems to obey no collective rules whatsoever. They are all commercially made, mass produced figures bought by the Art Department from dime stores in Los Angeles.

Several of the most memorable are, regrettably, still missing in action. But some have been saved for posterity.

All have been seen around the cockpit at one time or another, sometimes not so obviously, but they are there. As to which is where and when? Skip Crank, the on-set propmaster: "I used to have a big box of them and Joss and Alan Tudyk would reach in and choose their favorites for that day."

INARA'S PISTOL

EPISODE: 'TRASH'

'Trash' showed us Inara uncharacteristically brandishing not one, but two guns in a single episode, the Lassiter and this elegant, silver pistol.

It's based on a real-world firearm: the Ruger Mark 2 target pistol. This is a small caliber sporting piece, produced in both blued and nickel finishes. The black plastic grips are original. Although now legally deactivated, the action still functions and the pressed-steel magazine is removable.

There are two additions to the base gun which mark this prop as unique. The first is the machined aluminum suppressor/brake at the end of the muzzle. The brake is machined from a solid billet and has no aperture through which the gun could fire when live. It's screwed into place in a thread purpose-cut in the barrel.

The second addition is the outrigger/nacelle on the receiver. This piece is machined steel and features a working red light. It's secured in place with an Allen bolt, the thread tapped into a block mounted on the receiver.

In the hand the pistol is solid and weighty, but balanced and elegant. The machined add-ons do make the Ruger very sexy and sci-fi, but without taking us into the flamboyant, Golden Age of laser guns.

The pistol is contemporary and believable.

Elegant and beautiful, but still dangerous and business-like, this pistol is pure Inara.

JAYNE'S HOLD-OUT PIECE

EPSIODE: 'JAYNESTOWN'

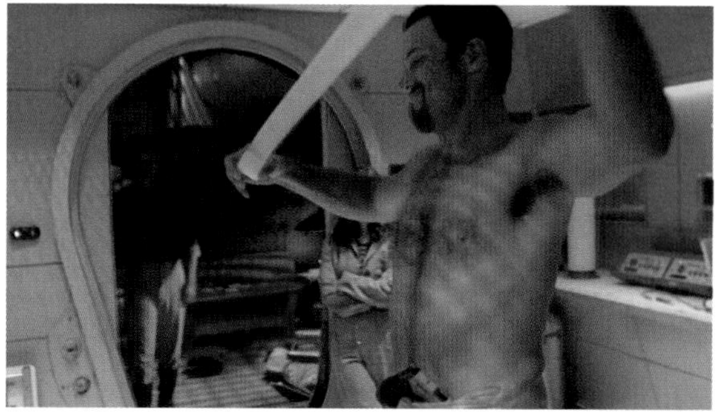

This interesting prop is glimpsed briefly in 'Jaynestown', being taped to Jayne's belly in the infirmary, before they touch down in Mudder central. Joss Whedon had spoken to propmaster Randy Eriksen about the need for Jayne to own an all-plastic gun, to avoid detection by sensors on Core planets. The prop was originally made as part of Jayne's bunk arsenal.

The design is interesting and the sharp-eyed will notice a more than passing similarity to Jubal Early's pistol. Perhaps both were made by the same prop maker.

The all-plastic pistol sports a set of black rubber Pachmayr grips, smaller than on the Early piece, and has graphite-colored holo-tape wrapping the barrel. The detailing is crisp and interesting, with at least a nod to functionality, whereas the Early pistol has no obvious controls at all.

The gun feels good in the hand. It's understandably light, but seems to point instinctively at the target, like the best real-world guns do.

Watching Jayne tape the gun industriously to his belly in 'Jaynestown' did raise a question though: how did he plan to draw it in a hurry?

SERENITY CONTROL KEYBOARD

MULTIPLE EPISODES

Part of the charm of the design of Serenity's interior sets is the attention to detail in the spit-and-bailing wire set dressing.

The Motorola KDT480 keyboard is an integral part of the look of the bridge. There are six in evidence there, ready to have their buttons frantically punched by a stressed out Wash.

Originally rented from a Hollywood prop house, and designed as part of a mobile computer terminal for police cruisers and fire trucks, the keyboards fit nicely into the jury-rigged design ethic of the Old Girl's bridge.

The KDT480 keyboard is also found on each and every one of the ship's interior com-panels. They also make a guest appearance in the Parcel office in 'The Message'.

The units feature an integral light bar at the top of the keyboard so the operator can use it in subdued lighting or even total darkness. As with most military/police equipment, the lighting is red. This is the only color of light which won't ruin your night vision. Often ship or aircraft controls are red lit for this purpose.

Many regional police and fire departments still use the system to this day.

ALAN TUDYK

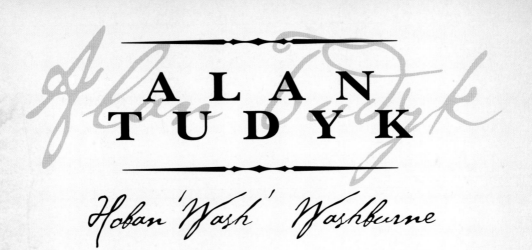

Hoban 'Wash' Washburne

ALAN ON MEETING THE FANS:
After *Firefly* was canceled, Nathan started going to conventions. I didn't. I didn't know what it [the fan experience] was about. Nathan talked me into it – I went to a convention in England. I could see there is a lot of passion there. But it's grown since then. I think *Firefly* fans are responsible for doing a lot of good.

INTERVIEW WITH ABBIE BERNSTEIN, 2009

NATHAN FILLION AND ALAN REMEMBER THE FIRST SCRIPT READ-THROUGH FOR THE SHOW:
Nathan: We did a table reading and I was sitting across from Alan Tudyk and he was being hilarious and self-deprecating and I'm a fan, and I'm like, "What is *he* doing here? He's a movie star, he's slumming!"
Alan: When I first got there and I was sitting around the table, I looked around and I thought, "I'm slumming, what am I doing here?" So [Nathan and I] we had that connection!"

SPEAKING ON STAGE AT THE 'SERENITY' CONVENTION, 2005.

ON MEETING GINA TORRES FOR THE FIRST TIME:

ALAN TUDYK

When I met Gina I was like [incredulous] "You're *my* wife? Wow, I really gotta step up here, how do I pull this off?"

SPEAKING ON STAGE AT THE 'SERENITY' CONVENTION, 2005.

ON HIS OPINION OF THE BIG DAMN MOVIE:
I loved the movie. I really liked the look of it, I liked the style of it, I thought Joss did a great job with it. There was one part of that movie where I was like, "Really?", which is where I *died*, but other than that, it was pretty awesome.

INTERVIEWED AT THE SUNDANCE FILM FESTIVAL, 2010

JEWEL STAITE ON ALAN'S MASTERY OF LANGUAGE:
Alan always screwed up his Chinese. He always came up with the most hilarious things to say just because he couldn't remember his lines and he thought he'd go with it. It was total gibberish in the end.

SPEAKING ON STAGE AT THE 'FUSION' CONVENTION, 2004.

NATHAN REMEMBERS HIS FAVORITE 'SLOW-COOKED' PRANK ON ALAN:
When we first did the pilot I made friends with everybody and Alan Tudyk was one of those people. I had to go to Vancouver for four weeks and do an independent film, and he was in Los Angeles looking for a place to live. I said, "You can live at my house, help feed my cat, for four weeks while you find your apartment," and it worked out great. And while he was at my house he left [behind] a calendar – it's one of those calendars where you go to the shopping mall and you get a bunch of family photos and you create a calendar putting one for each month. So it was family photos of him since he was a child. There were lots of really goofy photos of Alan Tudyk as a kid. So I saved it. I took all the goofiest pictures and I saved them for *three years*, and when we were doing the bar scene [in

the movie] I posted them all over the set – all these really, really goofy pictures of Alan. That made me happy!

SPEAKING ON STAGE AT 'THE WHITE ROOM' CONVENTION, 2004.

ON HIS HARDEST SCENE:

Any action scenes were easy for me, because I was on the ship [mimes sitting there, flicking a few switches]. The hardest one would have been when [Nathan and I] did 'War Stories'... our electrocution thing? My God... You tense your muscles and jiggle around... You try doing that for eight hours in a day, and see if you don't wake up the next day feeling like you were *actually* electrocuted.

SPEAKING ON STAGE AT DRAGON CON, 2008

NATHAN ON ALAN BEING PROTECTIVE OF THE BRIDGE SET:

If you changed the tilt on Alan's chair – look out! [As Alan] "Who was sitting in this... who did... If this isn't in the right... I'm not going to... If you guys don't... I'll be in my trailer!"

SPEAKING ON STAGE AT THE 'SERENITY' CONVENTION, 2005.

ALAN'S EPISODE IDEAS:

Ever since I started on *Firefly*, I've been pitching Joss Whedon ideas. One involves us capturing a bunch of wolves, to sell for like dog fights on a planet, but then River teaches the dogs peace, so they're no good... [Another idea] Inara has us as her servants, and somebody says "I need two strippers, can we use your servants?", and she's in a position where she has to say yes, and then we get sort of thrust into it. And Wash is really good – so you understand a bit more why Zoe and Wash are together, 'cause he's got *moves*.

INTERVIEWED ON SET, 2002

HE'S STILL AT IT...

I'm pitching to Joss Whedon a new TV show, it's not so much a series as a cycle, and I'm going to call it *The Wash Cycle*...

INTERVIEWED AT THE SUNDANCE FILM FESTIVAL, 2010

BEHIND THE SCENES

Danny Nero's Photo Album

When he first heard that *Firefly* was in pre-production, Danny Nero had spent three years on *Angel* as David Boreanaz's stand-in — the person who stands where the actor will be during a scene, so that lighting and camera moves can be planned without the actor having to be there in person during the often lengthy set up.

Nero explains, "As much as I enjoyed the people on *Angel*, the working conditions of so many nights in so many unsavory back alley locations in downtown LA... I thought, '*Firefly* is science fiction, which I love, and it's going to be a lot on a spaceship, which means being on a soundstage a lot, that's great.' I hadn't considered that we would have to go on location on *Firefly* occasionally, either to some of the local ranches or out into the desert, which would mean sometimes getting up at three in the morning to be there by six a.m. – but we enjoyed every minute on that show. It was such a fun place to work that we didn't mind going out to the desert every once in a while."

Nero's job was to stand in primarily for Nathan Fillion and occasionally for Adam Baldwin. "[Baldwin] is about six-six, and I'm about six-three, so three inches just about makes all the difference," Nero notes. "I was very lucky in that [original *Firefly* pilot costume designer] Jill Ohanneson found in Fox wardrobe a pair of Converse high-top tennis shoes that had six-inch platforms on them. I tried those on and people were in hysterics. I can't imagine why they were there, who would have used them on what show. I was in fear of falling and breaking something, so [Ohanneson] chopped off three inches, and I still have them to this day."

❖ Right: Danny Nero with Nathan Fillion.

❖ Below: with Adam Baldwin, on the set of 'The Message'.

When Fillion and Baldwin shared a scene, another stand-in would be brought in to work with Nero. "There might be a day where Nathan worked in the morning and Adam worked later on, so I could do both, but if they're both in the same scene, then you would have to have someone for each guy, and there was someone to cover each of the regular cast members. We had pretty much the same group of people the whole time. It was a great group all around, cast and crew, and it's always sad when that gets broken up."

Asked about particularly memorable days on set, Nero recalls, "Being out in the desert for a scene where Mal is completely naked. That required being at that desert location at least a full hour before the sun came up and it was quite cold. It was *very* cold." Fortunately, Nero was not called upon to be likewise bare. "No, I wore my closest flesh-colored clothes and I sat on that rock for a good bit of time before Nathan had to come out and do it. He was wearing something, but not very much, and he joked about it, but everyone was like, 'Oh, boy, there but for the grace of whoever ...'

"Because of Joss, people would do just about anything," Nero continues. "One day, I couldn't tell you what episode it was, but we were in one of the narrow corridors between the engine room and the dining room. And I don't know how it happened, but Joss started singing the song 'Oklahoma'. There were at least six or seven of us in there that all sang along and knew all the lyrics – including Nathan Fillion of course. We sang the entire theme song of *Oklahoma* and then just went around and continued working as if it had never happened," he laughs.

As for *Firefly* fandom, Nero says, "I would love to meet some of the fans. I never considered while I was working on it how popular the show would become. Of course, we never thought we would only do those few episodes, but we had no control over that. No one anticipated the fact that the DVD would help spawn a feature and that we would be doing that [Nero again stood in for Fillion and

Baldwin]. But once we were doing the feature, we were convinced, 'This will now spawn even more, there will be more features.' So it just goes to show you how you can never really be sure of anything in this business. Any time they're ready to get it back together and start the series up, I'd like to be involved somehow."

In the meantime, Nero still has his memories, and some great photos from his time on set...

Top: Filming 'The Message'.

Above: Nero with Jewel Staite, during filming for 'Shindig'.

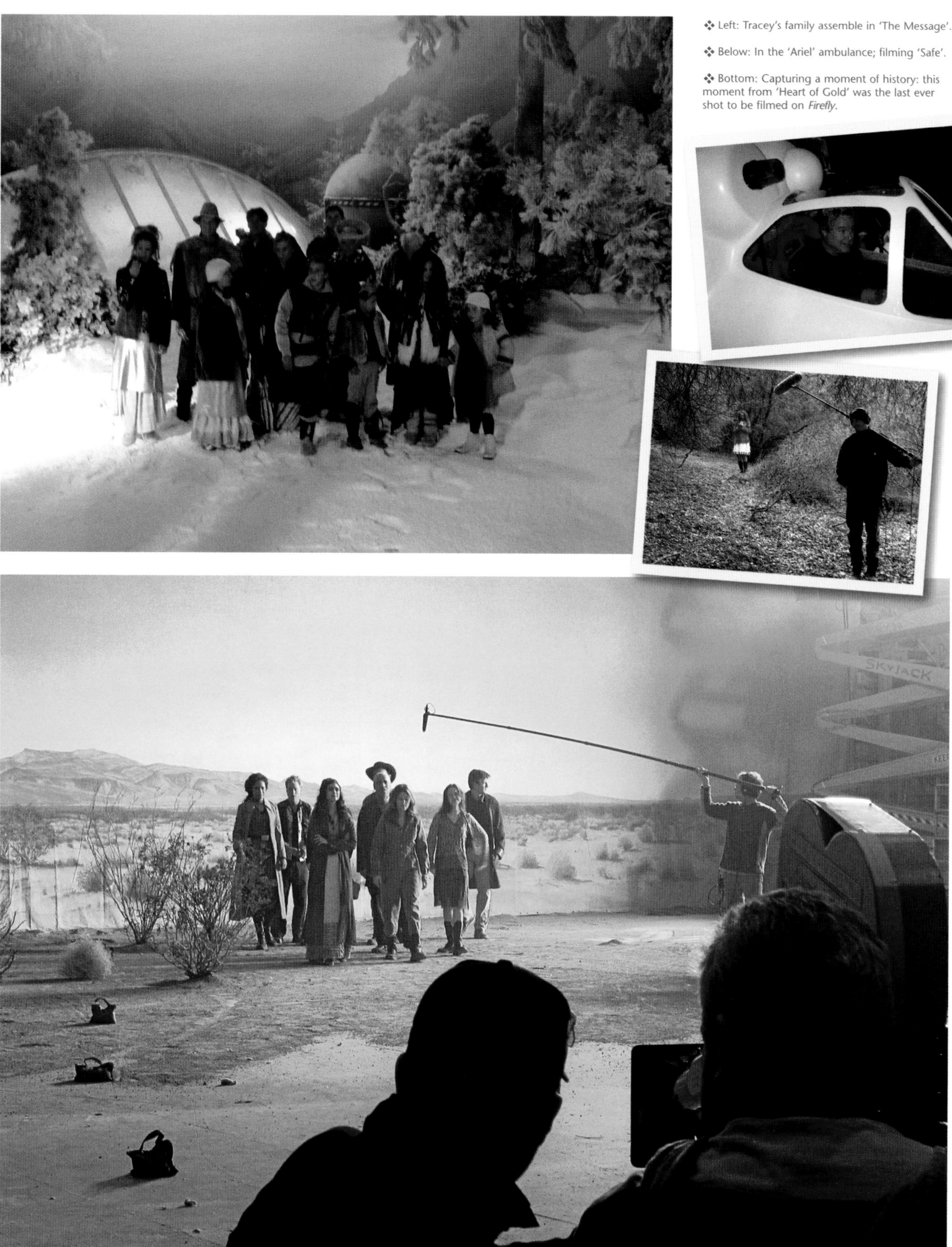

❖ Left: Tracey's family assemble in 'The Message'.

❖ Below: In the 'Ariel' ambulance; filming 'Safe'.

❖ Bottom: Capturing a moment of history: this moment from 'Heart of Gold' was the last ever shot to be filmed on *Firefly*.

❖ Top: Ron Glass says hello during filming for 'The Message'.

❖ Above: Shooting the opening scene of 'Ariel'.

❖ Far left center: Haymer's parlor from 'Trash'. The Lassiter is on the left.

❖ Far left bottom: Nero in front of the painted flat of Serenity, on location for 'Safe'.

❖ Left: Nero in costume as an extra for the ball scene in 'Shindig'.

❖ Top: Filming on the Serenity exterior set.

❖ Far right center: "No power in the 'verse can stop me." Filming 'War Stories'.

❖ Far right bottom: Nero in costume for 'The Message'.

❖ Right: Set detail. The sign warns of loud noise.

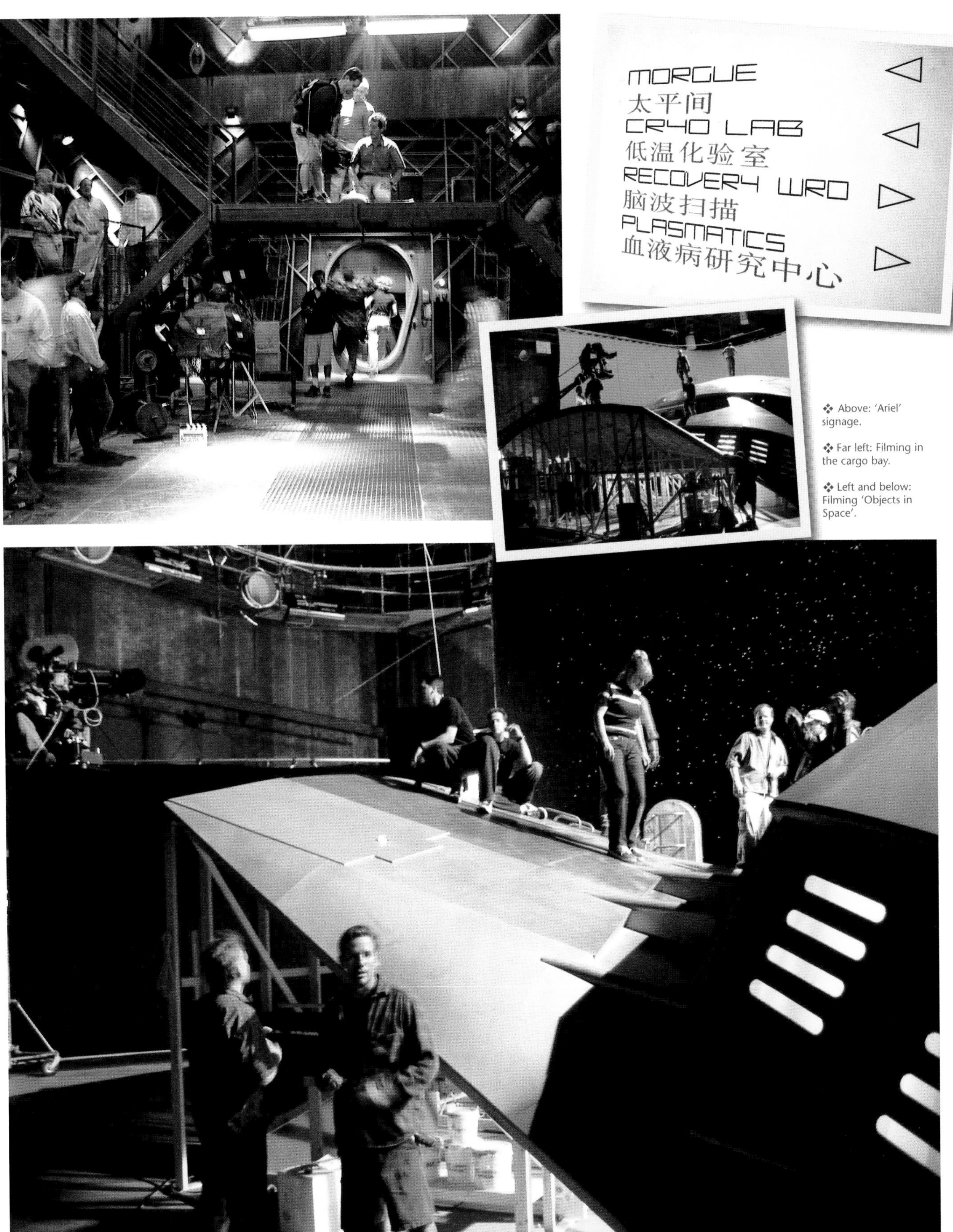

❖ Above: 'Ariel' signage.

❖ Far left: Filming in the cargo bay.

❖ Left and below: Filming 'Objects in Space'.

THE STORY OF MONKEY SHINES

The on-set practical joke that has passed into legend...

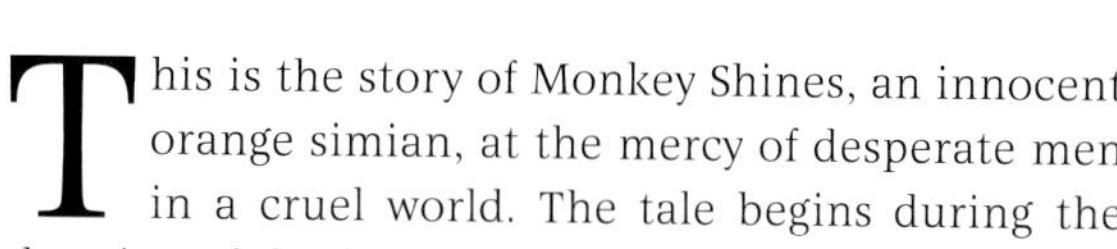

This is the story of Monkey Shines, an innocent orange simian, at the mercy of desperate men in a cruel world. The tale begins during the shooting of the first *Firefly* pilot show, 'Serenity'.

Propmasters standing-by on set often have a hand-wagon containing key props and set dressing for use in that day's scenes. Being a legendary practical joker, *Firefly* propmaster Skip Crank would tend to keep more esoteric items to hand as well: a small model of Han Solo in Carbonite for example, or realistic severed limbs, heads and body parts to surprise the cast with.

Skip had acquired a stuffed orange monkey toy with the most annoying screech known to man. The screech was so irritating in fact that eventually Joss Whedon banned the toy from the soundstage.

On this particular day, Skip was busy dressing the set for the upcoming scene and had left his wagon unattended. Not usually an issue, but a certain cast member was tired, a little cranky, and saw his chance...

This actor was between shooting some of the salvage scenes from the start of the episode and, rather than his usual tight pants, was dressed in one of Serenity's familiar khaki-colored space suits. He spotted Monkey Shines languishing on Skip's wagon and grabbed him, stuffing him down inside the suit and sauntering casually away.

Skip returned and was naturally distraught at the theft of his little buddy. He vowed to get him back.

What ensued is a very good example of what can happen when two imaginative, articulate and intelligent men have too much time on their hands...

This page, anti-clockwise from left:

❖ The poster that Skip made upon Monkey Shines' disappearance. Copies were posted all over the Fox Studio, soundstages and back-lot. The reference to *Mal*-nutrition shows he had his suspicions as to who the culprit may be, even at this stage.

❖ Several days after Monkey Shines' kidnapping, this envelope arrived on Skip's desk at the studio. The actor involved had taken to riding a small motor scooter around the lot. The tread on the tires is identical to that which made the muddy track across the envelope. More clues…

❖ This is the first of the ransom notes. It's clear the kidnapper is a desperate man. The pictures of the hapless Monkey Shines lashed to a chair are very moving. It is somewhat ironic that the word 'smart' is misspelled in the note.

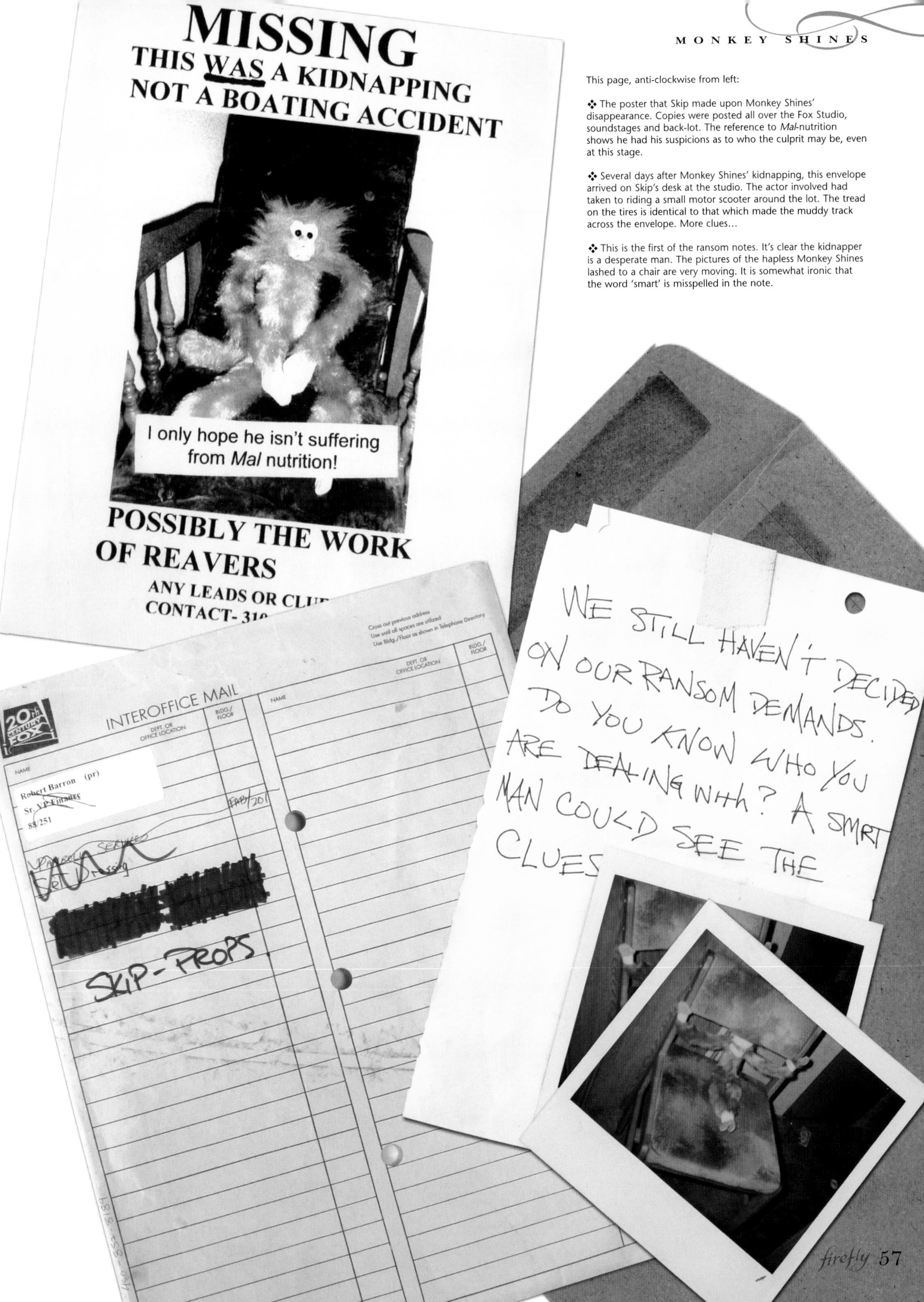

MISSING
THIS WAS A KIDNAPPING
NOT A BOATING ACCIDENT
I only hope he isn't suffering
from Mal nutrition!
POSSIBLY THE WORK
OF REAVERS
ANY LEADS OR CLU
CONTACT- 310
INTEROFFICE MAIL
20th CENTURY FOX
Robert Barron (pr)
Sr. VP Finance
88/251
SKIP - PROPS
WE STILL HAVEN'T DECIDED
ON OUR RANSOM DEMANDS.
DO YOU KNOW WHO YOU
ARE DEALING WITH? A SMRT
MAN COULD SEE THE
CLUES

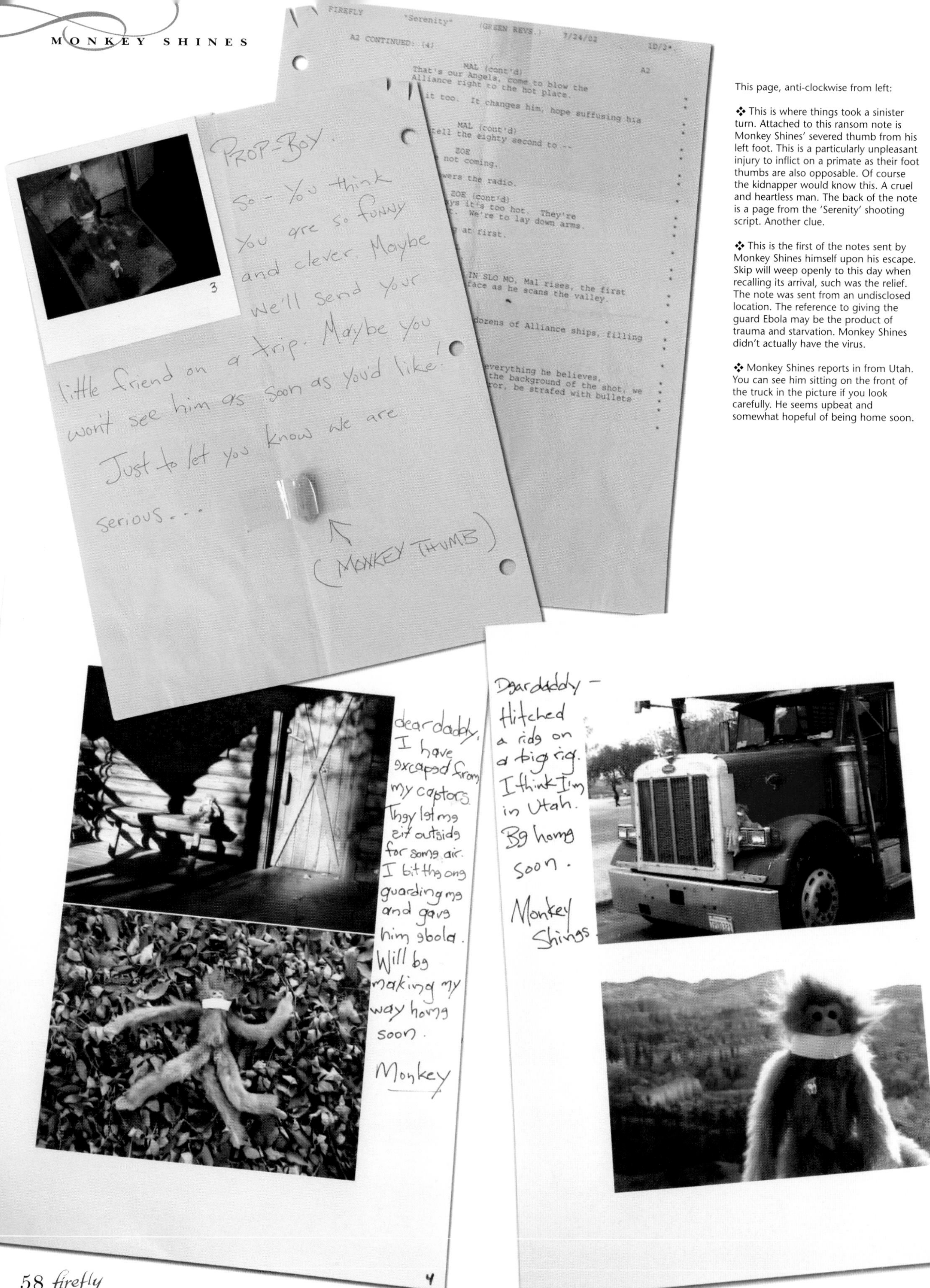
FIREFLY "Serenity" (GREEN REVS.) 7/24/02
A2 CONTINUED: (4) 1D/2*.

MAL (cont'd) A2
That's our Angels, come to blow the
Alliance right to the hot place.

it too. It changes him, hope suffusing his

MAL (cont'd)
tell the eighty second to --

ZOE
not coming.

wers the radio.

ZOE (cont'd)
ys it's too hot. They're
. We're to lay down arms.

at first.

IN SLO MO, Mal rises, the first
face as he scans the valley.

dozens of Alliance ships, filling

everything he believes,
the background of the shot, we
ror, be strafed with bullets

3

PROP-BOY.
So - You think
You are so funny
and clever. Maybe
we'll send your
little friend on a trip. Maybe you
won't see him as soon as you'd like!
Just to let you know we are
serious...
(MONKEY THUMB)

dear daddy,
I have
excaped from
my captors.
They let me
eit outside
for some air.
I bit the one
guarding me
and gave
him ebola.
Will be
making my
way home
soon.
Monkey

4

Dear daddy -
Hitched
a ride on
a big rig.
I think I'm
in Utah.
Be home
soon.
Monkey
Shines

This page, anti-clockwise from left:

❖ This is where things took a sinister turn. Attached to this ransom note is Monkey Shines' severed thumb from his left foot. This is a particularly unpleasant injury to inflict on a primate as their foot thumbs are also opposable. Of course the kidnapper would know this. A cruel and heartless man. The back of the note is a page from the 'Serenity' shooting script. Another clue.

❖ This is the first of the notes sent by Monkey Shines himself upon his escape. Skip will weep openly to this day when recalling its arrival, such was the relief. The note was sent from an undisclosed location. The reference to giving the guard Ebola may be the product of trauma and starvation. Monkey Shines didn't actually have the virus.

❖ Monkey Shines reports in from Utah. You can see him sitting on the front of the truck in the picture if you look carefully. He seems upbeat and somewhat hopeful of being home soon.

❖ Top left: Another update from the brave little fellow. Why he's lashed to the post is a bit of a mystery. The psychological effects of malnutrition may be a factor.

❖ Left: It seems he was a little addled and ended up back in Utah again. Definitely something amiss here. On the upside, he seems positive. Almost chipper.

dear daddy - Getting closer. finding food where i can. Raided campground. Slowed down in Washington, long story.
dear daddy - This nice lady (who wishes to remain nameless) helped me get home by mailing me from Canada. I'm home!
Monkey Shines.

This page, clockwise from above:

❖ Monkey Shines seems to be back on track. He's managed to find a banana in a Washington campground. Although now properly nourished, he still seems somewhat confused. The self-imposed gag may be a silent cry for help.

❖ Rescued and posted home by a nice lady from Alberta, Canada.

❖ Skip was overjoyed to see Monkey Shines alive and well, and alerted the media. Monkey Shines himself, psychologically and emotionally bruised by the ordeal, was operating on his own agenda.

❖ This candid and somewhat unsettling shot was taken by Skip while visiting his friend during his recovery. It seems Monkey Shines was not willing to let bygones be bygones and seemed intent on revenge. The need for retribution reached obsessive levels and Monkey Shines was eventually taken into care for his own protection. He now resides in a peaceful rest home for damaged toys in West London, England.

DAILY VARIETY

Reed Business Information

LOS ANGELES ■ NEW YORK

$3.25 NEWSPAPER

WEDNESDAY NOVEMBER 19, 2003

VARIETY.COM

AMC, Loews eyeing major screen team

...RL DIORIO

...ws Cineplex are in talks about a ...liminary agreement by year's end. ...the No. 1 and No. 5 U.S. exhibs ...ore than 5,600 screens. That's ...egal amassed by combining ...couple years, but its big... Regal's.

...nt to the studios, because ...said Bryan Krug, an an... ...Overland Park, Kan. ...was unclear whether a ...right or a transaction ...equity position. ...s over the years, ...ent discussions, ...ugh real estate ...rty portfolio.

...urn to page 16

MONKEY SURFACES!

Simian Vows Vengeance for Kidnappings

NBC and CBS remain locked in a down-to-the-wire, bare-knuckle battle for sweeps bragging rights — but ABC picked up some steam last week as the key ratings frame headed into the home stretch.

Fox, however, was well behind its rivals despite remaining on top in some of the younger demo categories. Net's in much better shape relative to the other major nets vs. a year ago, though, and is hopeful for another second-half rally once "American Idol" arrives in January.

...10-16, NBC's 4.3 rating/12 share in adults 18-49 — although it reps a troubling 16% decline from the net's perf in the same week a year ago — was enough to hold off CBS and ABC, which tied at 4.0/11, and was a full ratings point ahead of Fox's 3.3/9.

Through 19 nights of the four-week November sweep, NBC (4.4/12) remained on top in adults 18-49, but was down 14% year-to-year. Net was followed by CBS (4.2/12, up 2%), ABC (3.6/10, down 8%), Fox (3.1/8, down 11%).

CBS has the advantage over runner-up NBC in both adults 25-54 (5.4/13 to 5.0/12) and total viewers (14.84 million to 11.40m).

Meanwhile, there are some new season-to-date leaders through eight weeks of the season in categories that figure to get tight in the second half of the season: NBC has overtaken baseball-boosted Fox in adults 18-49 (4.3/12 vs. 4.2/12) and CBS now is on top in adults 25-54 (5.0/12), inching ahead of NBC (4.9/12).

Turn to page 15

THE KIDNAPPER... REVEALED!

NATHAN FILLION CONFESSES ALL

There was a monkey on set and if you squeezed it, it made this monkey noise. It was fine enough, but once you've heard it more than once, it got a little annoying. I had to wear a space suit all day and that's the worst. You're claustrophobic, you're sweating and Sean Maher had to wear it before me because we didn't have enough space suits to go around. The space suit was sweaty and hot and it's awful. Sean's worked all day and he takes it and hands it to me and he says, "Sorry." And there's nothing you can do, and I say, "No problem man." So I'm getting into an already hot and sweaty space suit and it's claustrophobic and you can't really hear anybody, and everybody is tugging on it to get you in it and everyone is smacking you around... It had to weigh about 120, 130 pounds. I hated it. I loved that job, but if you wanted to see me with a sour face and all cranky, put me in a space suit.

And that damn monkey would not shut up.

So when I left I pulled up my helmet, grabbed the monkey and shoved him in my spacesuit, walked back to my trailer and hid him in a drawer. Then I took a Polaroid camera and I taped up the monkey's eyes and his mouth, taped him to a chair and started taking Polaroids of him, with little items in the back as clues as to who it would be that stole him. Of course they recognized my trailer in the photos! Not too bright. One too many knocks with the helmet. So they put out an ad saying that they hoped the monkey wasn't Mal-nourished. Then I wrote a letter back to them – a ransom note with the monkey's thumb taped to it saying, "Quit messing around." Then I mailed the monkey to my parents, who took it on a cross-country trip across Canada and into the States, and took pictures of this monkey all over [yes, that's Nathan's mother in the picture opposite]. Then I finally returned the monkey...

SPEAKING ON STAGE AT THE 'WHITE ROOM' CONVENTION, 2004

MORENA BACCARIN

Inara Serra

MORENA ON THE FEEDBACK SHE GETS FROM FANS:

They have a very mutual understanding of the work, I think. They really enjoy the same things that we enjoy in it. They have such an in-depth understanding of the world, the universe that was created. They really do their research, and they read things about it. They're very intelligent. And they're really passionate about it. They get really into the world, and they dress up as us sometimes. They have these really intelligent questions about the Alliance vs. the Browncoats, it's really cool.

INTERVIEW WITH ZETAMINOR.COM, 2005

ON THE FANS:

I still can't believe that people were as into that show as they were, and are. It's great and I loved the series, because I was in it and working and loved the people that I worked with. I am always amazed and humbled by the amount of fans out there for *Firefly* and it's so touching to me that people feel as passionately about it as I did.

Just the other day I went to eat in a restaurant here in Los Angeles, and the owners were huge *Firefly* fans wearing *Serenity* shirts. I had no idea and told the owner that I liked her shirt and she said, "Oh my God, I was hoping one of you would come in eventually!" It's so great. It's so sweet.

INTERVIEW WITH IFMAGAZINE.COM, 2007

ON INARA'S SHUTTLE SET:

Morena: My room was kind of great because nobody ever came in it except Nathan, and then we just bickered and he would storm out. I had it all to myself.

Nathan: Actually when we weren't filming, I twice went in there for a nap.

SPEAKING ON STAGE AT THE 'SERENITY' CONVENTION, 2005

ON JOINING THE SHOW AFTER EVERYONE ELSE HAD BEEN CAST:

I felt that everybody was leagues ahead of me and I was just playing catch up the whole time, but my first

impression of Joss was kind of funny. I read for the casting director first and she said, "OK Joss is downstairs on set we'll get him up," because they were rushing to get this going. And he comes in and he's got a hat on and a ragged T-shirt and a beard and he's like, "Hi" and I was like, "Who is this guy? How is he directing this and what is this person in front of me?" And he started talking, and I hadn't even read the script at that point, I hadn't had any time, and I thought, "Oh my god I will do anything this man does. It doesn't matter what my part is. I know I can trust him and I know that I'm in good hands." That kicked it off really well.

SPEAKING ON STAGE AT THE 'SERENITY' CONVENTION, 2005

JEWEL STAITE ON MORENA:

Morena and I got really, really close very quickly. We have like the same birthday on the same day. We were just like two peas in a pod. She was the maid of honor at my wedding and we just became really, really close. But we would say mean, horrible things to each other in front of people, just to get a reaction. We were in this room full of extras on 'Shindig' and there was just this lull, this silent moment and she turned around and she looked at me and she said, "I am so sick of looking at your face." Everyone was like [mimes shock] and I just burst out laughing.

SPEAKING ON STAGE AT THE 'SERENITY' CONVENTION, 2005

MORENA AND NATHAN ON INARA'S RELATIONSHIP WITH MAL:

Morena: You can see in 'Out of Gas' they met when she was looking for shuttles to rent, and right away you can tell that they're attracted to each other. Not necessarily in a sexual way, but there is something which brings them together, and the minute he calls her a whore – it's all downhill.

Nathan: I think that Malcolm Reynolds pegged her right off the bat seeing that she's running away from something.

Morena: Takes one to know one!

SPEAKING ON STAGE AT 'THE WHITE ROOM' CONVENTION, 2005

ON HER FAVORITE EPISODE:

Maybe it was 'Shindig'. One of the most satisfying things for me, apart from watching Nathan get the crap kicked out of him [laughs] – well, it doesn't suck to be a girl and wear pretty dresses and have two guys fight over you.

SPEAKING ON STAGE AT 'THE WHITE ROOM' CONVENTION, 2005

ON GIFTS FROM FANS:

I didn't get this as a gift, but Christina Hendricks did. She received coasters with all of our faces on them, so she gets a really big kick whenever I go to her house giving me the coaster with my face on it, so I can put a glass on top of it.

INTERVIEW WITH IFMAGAZINE.COM, 2007

COSTUMES

Selections from the wardrobes of Inara and Jayne

❖ Opposite: The design for Inara's costume from 'Ariel'.

❖ This page top right: Inara's dress for 'Shindig' was adapted from Shawna Trpcic's own wedding dress.

❖ This page right: The design for a costume seen in 'War Stories'.

❖ Below: Shawna Trpcic at San Diego Comic-Con 2009.

❖ Overleaf: Jayne's iconic T-shirts and hat. Kept by Adam Baldwin after filming ended, he later auctioned them off, raising thousands of dollars for charity.

FIREFLY COSTUME DESIGNER SHAWNA TRPCIC

I went and spoke at Comic-Con this year, at the Browncoat panel, and as I was answering questions about the *Firefly* costumes, we also did a flashpoint [presentation] of the Jayne hats and sang 'A Man Called Jayne'. Also, Nathan Fillion came in right in the middle of the interview – big hugs and kisses and it was awesome. I saw many replicas at Comic-Con, after almost six years, of the Browncoat Mal outfit.

INTERVIEW WITH ABBIE BERNSTEIN, 2009

INARA going to core hospital
ep 8
sleeve
larger to hang
COSTUME DESIGNERS GUILD
IATSE
892
494
= INARA'S sweatsuit =

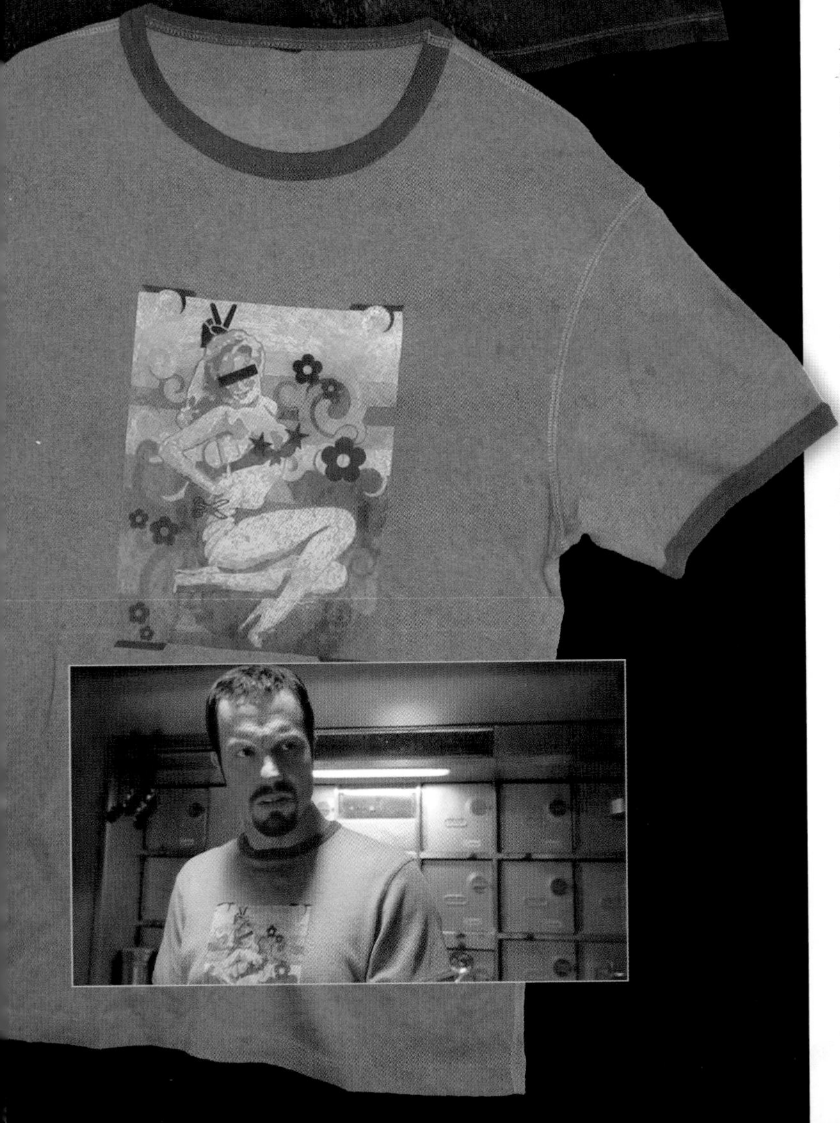

ADAM BALDWIN ON THAT CUNNING-LOOKING GIFT FROM JAYNE'S MOM:

It was very much of sentimental value for Jayne. We haven't met his mom yet, but I always pictured her as someone short and feisty, like Ruth Gordon, that Jayne could carry around in his arms... [The hat has] a lot of sentimental value for me. I love it, I think it's great [seeing fans wear it at conventions]. It stands out. It really pops!

INTERVIEW WITH HYPA SPACE, 2006

ADAM BALDWIN

Jayne Cobb

ADAM ON THE CHARACTER'S APPEAL:

Jayne is this guy who says what everybody wishes they could say. He's that big elephant in the room that will just spew the truth and I think people relate to that... Joss gave me some really fun words to say and I just got to drop my voice [in Jayne's gruff tones] *like this.*

INTERVIEW WITH ZETAMINOR.COM, 2005

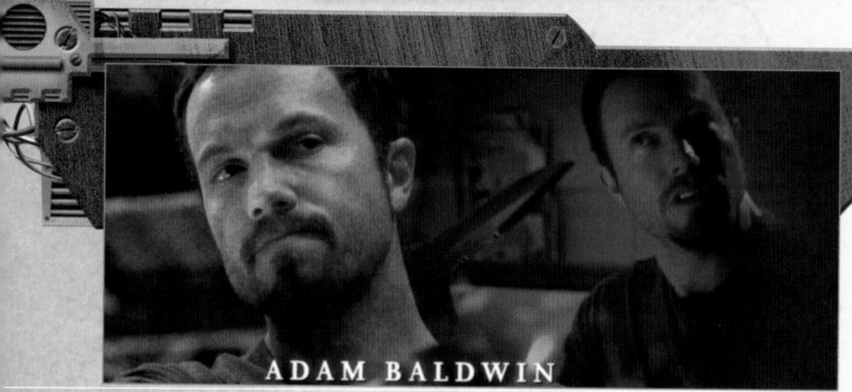

ADAM BALDWIN

ON HIS INSPIRATION:

I had just been trying to do Warren Oates from *The Wild Bunch* meets Eli Wallach from *The Good, the Bad and the Ugly*. Guys like that. Those are guys I was trying to impersonate, mixed in with some Strother Martin. Those are great Western guys. I just always approached it as a Western, with that sensibility. You can shoot someone in the back and rationalize it, because you're out on the frontier, and survival of the fittest. It was up to Joss to infuse him with a little bit of a heart of gold and honor for Mal. The rest of them, he could take or leave them. And later I saw *Alien* again, and it turns out I was just doing Yaphet Kotto.

INTERVIEW WITH THE ONION A.V. CLUB, 2009

ON COMING BACK FOR THE MOVIE:

It fit like a glove. I still had the boots from the series. I slipped right back into those, and a couple of the T-shirts. We upgraded them a little bit, and put on some cooler beltwork and weaponry. The gun sling that the prop guy made for the movie used a quick-release parachute capo. That was pretty cool. It was great to have that group back again, because at that point, we all appreciated what it was. It was probably the most fun job I've ever worked on. It was so sweet. Such redemption. I'm sorry the movie didn't make more money at the theaters. If we'd had three more million viewers for the show, we'd still be on the air, and if we'd had three million more butts in the seats, we'd probably have made a sequel or two.

INTERVIEW WITH THE ONION A.V. CLUB, 2009

ON WHETHER JAYNE HAD A CRUSH ON INARA:

It wasn't that tough [to play that]! I've been to a couple of panel discussions with Morena, and I've mentioned that, and she said, "Do you have a crush on me?" And I'm like... "Nah... my character does though." But Joss

would say, "No, you don't have a crush on Inara!" "Yes I do. I don't care what you say, I'm going to play it!"
I love those guys. It was really a family affair. It's so rare to have a cast like that.

SPEAKING ON STAGE AT A CONVENTION, 2005

ON JAYNE IN 'ARIEL', AND THE QUALITY OF THE WRITING:

Even though he's a bit of a ne'er do well, that's the realm into which he's painted, but he has that sort of honor among thieves. Even in the episode in the series where I quote unquote 'betrayed' the Captain by trying to dump off the loony fugitives ['Ariel'] – in my own mind, I wasn't betraying the Captain, I was trying to do better and just make a buck along the way. When he clocked me in the head with a wrench – "Hello, now I'm awake. OK, I get it now."

I think what that shows is Joss's brilliance. I think that shows his ability to connect with an audience in writing profound stories, with action and quite a bit of sense of humor, that are universal in nature. That touch people across a wide spectrum of age ranges. I'm not saying that he has the most gigantic audience in the world, but the audience that he has is very varied. You can't put them in a box you know — young and old, men and women, freaks and geeks — you got 'em all. I'm just happy to be part of that world. I'm so proud to have been given... I think it's a role of a lifetime.

INTERVIEW WITH SMRT-TV.COM, 2005

ON WHAT JAYNE COBB AND JOHN CASEY (HIS CHARACTER IN *CHUCK*) WOULD TALK ABOUT IF THEY MET:

"Weaponry first, hot girls second."

INTERVIEW WITH JOHN PATRICK BARRY, 2010

"Port Control is paying four credits for every stray we kill!"

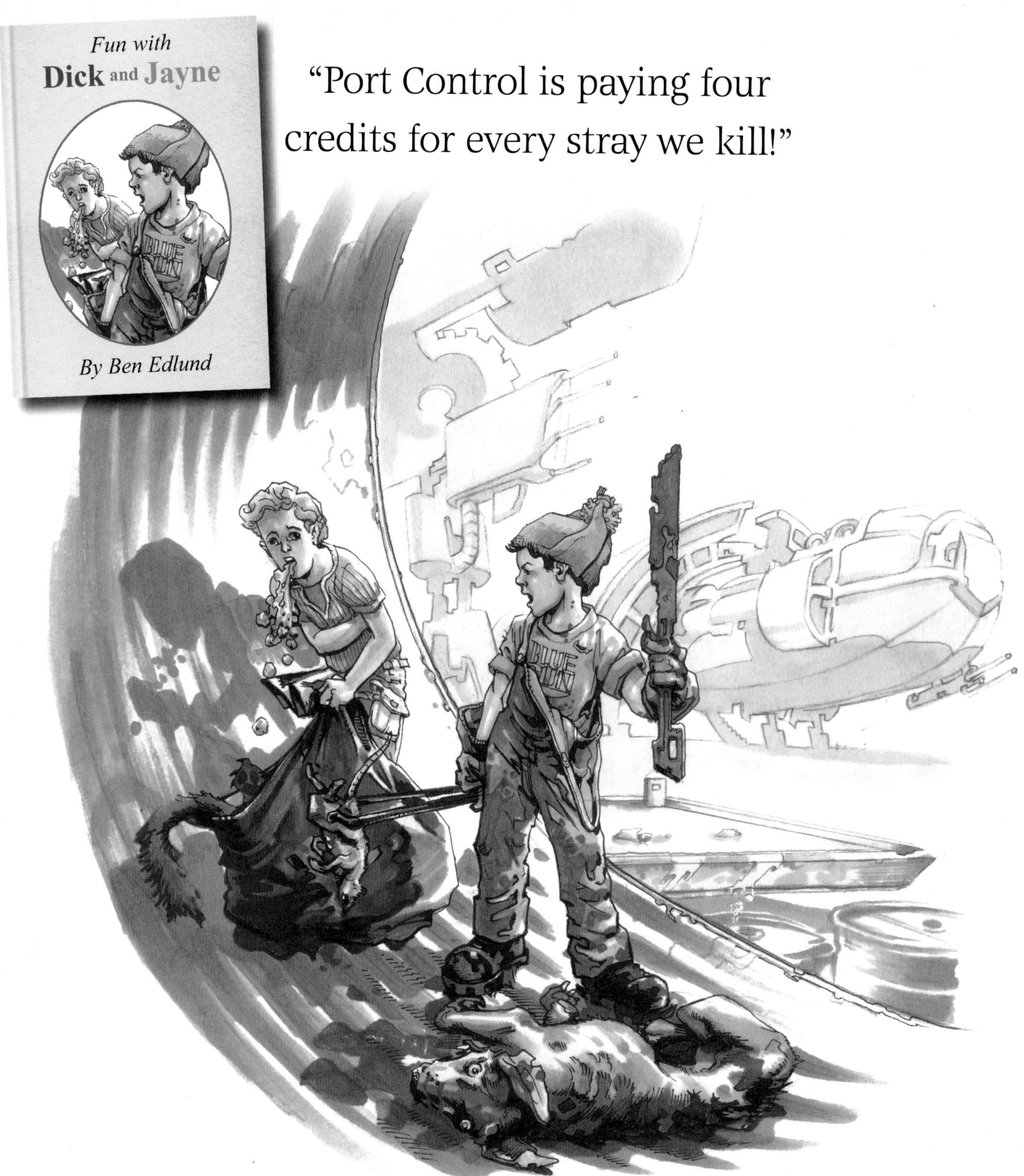

"Stop it, Dick," says Jayne. "Stop it."

"Now we have enough money to back our own hobo in the Meat Raffle!"

"Sic'em, Speshal!" shouts Jayne. "Yay!"

THE HEAD THEY CALL JAYNE

Whatever happened to the Jaynestown statue?

One of the more memorable pieces of *Firefly* set dressing was the statue of Jayne created for 'Jaynestown'. Mike Schotte of Dallas, Texas, wound up in possession of the statue's head.

"Adam Baldwin brought it as a charity auction item for the Flanvention [held in Burbank, California in 2005]," Schotte relates. "It's in good shape. Basically, at the end of the day's shooting, he broke the head off the body of the statue and took it home! Then the production office called him and said they had to do some pick-up shots, so they had to put it back together, which is why it's got a pole in the head, so they could stick it back on. If you look in the episode, you can see the crack around the head in some of the shots. During opening ceremonies of the Flanvention, they mentioned the charity auction, which they hadn't said much about, but Adam just said, 'Oh, by the way, I brought the Jayne statue.' I immediately freaked out, went and found money. It is just an iconic prop. I mean, that's so obviously *Firefly*. There were a lot of great things there, but that was something that I just said, 'I'm going to go for it and do whatever I can to get it.'"

It's been challenging to place such a unique item within a household. "It's kind of a hard thing to display," Schotte acknowledges. "Right now, it's packed away safely. I've been trying for years and years to research if the rest of it was out there anywhere. But everybody I've talked to has basically said that they think that the body went into the trash at the end of shooting. I went to Mutant Enemy Strike Day [organized by Joss Whedon in support of the 2007/2008 Writers Guild of America strike], and Jane Espenson introduced me to Joss. Since I just ask everybody, I said, 'Somebody told me there was a rumor that you might have the Jayne statue in your garage.' He said, 'Nope, that's not true.' I said, 'Yeah, I figured it probably wasn't true. Who's going to keep a headless body in their garage for five years?' He said, 'Well, I didn't say I didn't have *any* headless bodies, just not that one,'" Schotte laughs.

"I know the special effects house, Almost Human, who made the statue, and I talked to Shawna Trpcic, who provided the clothing for when they made the statue, but I haven't been able to track down any more pieces of it."

Schotte does have at least one complementary piece of memorabilia. "When Adam sold his shooting scripts in charity auctions, I bought his 'Jaynestown' script to go with the head, and his notes that he's written in the margin crack me up. Next to Jayne's line, 'The magistrate of this company town ain't exactly a forgiving sort of fella,' he's written in the margin, 'We're all going to die a horrible muddy death.' That alone makes it worth the price."

❖ Opposite top: The Jaynestown statue, as immortalized in a poster produced by QMx.

JAYNESTOWN

CANTON

JEWEL STAITE

Kaywinnit Lee Frye

JEWEL ON GETTING READY TO PLAY KAYLEE:

When I first auditioned for *Firefly*, I read the breakdown of the characters and the one that caught my eye was River. I read it and I thought, "Oh that sounds meaty, I like that." There was a lot of crying and hysteria and every actor wants to do that. But then I read Kaylee, and they said, "Well actually Joss wants to see you for Kaylee," and I thought "Oh," because it said "chubby" on the breakdown, and I'm not chubby, and I didn't know if they meant 'Hollywood chubby' or what. So I put myself on tape and kind of forgot about it, and then a few weeks later I got the call and I flew down to meet Joss, and he told me flat out. He said, "You know I need this character to be full of life, and by full of life I mean she has to look like she enjoys life. She has to look like she eats a burger now and then, and drinks a few beers once in a while." He didn't want her to be a typical size zero actress, which I understand. I'm naturally this way. I was a little taken aback because I'm really into yoga, and I like to stay healthy. But I loved the role so much it wasn't like I was going to say no. So I just stuffed my face for about three weeks, and got to eat lots of mayonnaise. I got to eat doughnuts every morning and I felt so sick because I was so full all the time, but I had to keep eating like that to keep the weight on. It was interesting. My husband loved it – guys apparently like a little weight on women! It was awesome.

SPEAKING ON STAGE AT THE 'FUSION' CONVENTION, 2004

ON THE EVOLUTION OF THE CHARACTER:

Once I had the part and we started to shoot, it was a bit unclear how bubbly Kaylee was supposed to be. Is she just happy or is she more manic? Is she hiding something and that's why she puts on the happy facade, or is she just drunk? I figured the best route to go was to play up her innocence, her frankness, and her warmth more than anything. 'Out of Gas' put me straight on the whole innocence thing, so after that I added horny flirt to her repertoire.

INTERVIEW WITH RAYGUNREVIVAL.COM, 2007

ON KAYLEE'S LIFE BEFORE JOINING THE SERENITY CREW:

I did a bit of imagining, but I also trusted Joss with any kind of backstory questions I had. I knew she had a great family, maybe not such a well-off one, but a family that was supportive of her and her abilities, otherwise why would they have let her go with someone like Mal? That's one of the things that was most disappointing for me when the series got canceled so prematurely; I would have loved to learn more about her life off the ship... I would have loved to meet her family. I've always had this desire to see Kaylee become a mother. She's child-like in a lot of ways, but also loving and maternal. I think she would have been a really great mom.

INTERVIEW WITH RAYGUNREVIVAL.COM, 2007

ON 'JOSS SPEAK':

Once I got used to it, it became really easy. I can't help myself doing it off set, that broken English he sometimes writes for us.

INTERVIEW WITH ZETAMINOR.COM, 2005

ON HER HARDEST SCENE TO SHOOT:

The hardest for me was probably the one in 'Objects in Space', in the engine room with Early, even though he [Richard Brooks] was a very nice man. That was a tough day at work. The not-hardest was any time I had to make out with Sean. Just being honest! He smells *beautiful*.

SPEAKING ON STAGE AT DRAGON CON, 2008

ON HER FEELINGS TOWARDS THE SHOW:

I had such a love affair with this show in a really crazy, mad way. I still watch the episodes when I'm feeling glum, and just the fact that we got to do the movie and that we got to work together again and that being canceled wasn't the end was so incredible.

SPEAKING ON STAGE AT THE 'SERENITY' CONVENTION, 2005

ON FOREVER BEING KNOWN AS THE 'SMUDGY, SMILEY MECHANIC'.

It's kind of funny: I've met some fans at certain events and conventions and things who say I look "sooooo much better" with grease on my face and overalls on. Like, thanks. But at least she's a likeable character! I never imagined when I signed on to *Firefly* that this would happen. I think we all knew from the very beginning that we were creating something quite special, so when I meet people that understand and appreciate it, it feels really nice. The whole experience holds a lot of wonderful memories for me. Like when Nathan put hand lotion under the door handles of my trailer and laughed at me when I fell down the stairs. Other than that, I love all those guys, and I miss them a lot.

INTERVIEW WITH RAYGUNREVIVAL.COM, 2007

THRILLING HEROICS

Stunts

An interview with Firefly Stunt Coordinator Nick Brandon

Australian-accented Nick Brandon was born in Singapore, where he studied martial arts as a youth. He refined his craft in the Hong Kong film industry, then moved to the US and began doing stunts in Hollywood. "I decided this is where it was happening," Brandon laughs. As he grew more experienced, he began dividing his time between doing stunts and stunt coordination. He worked for Mutant Enemy on both *Buffy the Vampire Slayer* and *Angel*. *Angel* stunt coordinator Mike Massa suggested Brandon for the *Firefly* gig after Eddie Braun had coordinated the pilot, 'Serenity'.

ON THE GENERAL STYLE OF *FIREFLY* STUNTS:

I didn't want to go too Hong Kong *Matrix*-y. I tried to blend more of a powerful, almost a realistic look with some of the Hong Kong stuff and also with the kind of lifelike fights that happen a lot in English film and television. The fighting styles developed based on the characters, how they moved and what would work out best for them, so basically it grew with them.

The *Firefly* regulars were all great, they were all very physical. The main two that I worked with were Nathan and Adam. They both have their own styles that developed, Adam being a lot more powerful-looking in his style of fighting; Nathan is very talented in most of the things he does. They were both awesome to work with, very easy.

ON 'THE TRAIN JOB':

We had a stunt where we had Adam's stunt double Tim Sitarz jump out of the spaceship and land on the roof of the train. He jumped out of the full-sized spaceship into a hole, basically. We put a green screen down below, so he jumped out onto pads, out of the full-sized ship.

For the second part of the stunt, we had one or two carriages of the train that we built on stage that I landed him down on. He was actually suspended in mid-air on a wire that just released and then decelerated him as he lands on top of the carriage.

When Mal kicks Crow into the engine, that was actually done CG. They scanned the actor [Andrew Bryniarski] and then used a completely computer-generated character that flew into the engine. I had ideas of how to do it practically; time was probably the reason that they went with purely CG. The kick was for real. We just cut out of him as soon as he started to go backwards. He hardly went backwards at all. As soon as the kick happened, they cut out of it.

ON 'SHINDIG':

In the story, Mal couldn't swordfight at all. Atherton Wing [played by Edward Atterton], who challenged him to the duel, was supposedly an expert sword-fighter. It was interesting to do a swordfight where one person's obviously not very skilled and the other person is an expert. In reality, the actors were both very good. Nathan was great. I brought in a sword guy, Tim Weske, to help choreograph the sword stuff and work with the actors on getting them up to scratch sword-wise. Pretty much, I'll give him the outline of the fight, the important beats and then see what he comes up with. The stunt doubles did quite a bit of the sword-fighting stuff. Usually, you film over the shoulder of one guy looking at the other guy, and the guy you're looking at is going to be the actor and you're over the shoulder of the stunt double. The stunt double is really accurate, so they can get really close to the actor with their moves, and they can make it look great.

ON 'SAFE':
There was a gun battle with a few stunt people in that. Generally speaking, if they're not actors, i.e., if they're just nondescript people in the scenes who come in and have a gun battle, they'll be stunt people. We'll talk about it and it'll be, "You come around the corner and this guy shoots you, you take a hit here," and the director will require a squib hit, a blood pack, so special effects will work that out and then we'll do our part of it. All the stunt people I hire would know how to take any of those kinds of hits and go to the ground, no problem. Where the hits are on the body will be up to the director. A lot of times, that'll be decided in a pre-production meeting, so it will be known by everybody way beforehand.

ON 'JAYNESTOWN':
There was a bit where a guy jumped in front of a shotgun blast. That was in fact a stunt double, although you do see his face. I put him on a wire to change his direction in mid-air, so he actually dove in front heading one way, and as he got hit, spun around and landed. When wire stunts are done outdoors, you can go with anything to hold the wire, from cranes to great forklift pieces of machinery of adjustable height, that weigh a lot. Basically, you're looking for anything solid!

ON 'ARIEL':

I played the guard who was taking them in. That was actually me and Adam who did that fight. Because Jayne had his hands handcuffed behind him, I choreographed this fight that involved him doing certain things. There's fighting and gouging and it was intense, because story-wise, Jayne had to stop the guard from screaming and alerting the other guards that there was something happening. So the whole time he's fighting, he's also trying to stop the guard from screaming. I wanted it to be a really intense, strong, nasty fight. I was trying to think of somebody I could use as the guard, and the more I started choreographing it and thinking about it, I realized, "Well, by the time I've explained exactly what I want to somebody, and try and get him to do exactly what I want, maybe I'll just do it myself!" And Adam was great in that scene.

ON 'TRASH':

I think the biggest mishap we had was [Jayne double] Tim Sitarz, who hit his head doing the stunt on 'Trash'. We did a wire thing as one of the containers explodes and throws him back. He landed on the outside of the ship. He went backwards about ten, twelve feet, something like that. In that instance, a cable went up to the perms [permanent cable-bearing fixtures] on the stage and then down to a ratchet, the piece of machinery that pulled him backwards. The wire was attached to a harness that he's wearing underneath his wardrobe. In that case, it was attached to his back. When we pulled him backwards, he basically whipped back and hit the back of his head. He went and got it checked out though, and he was fine.

ON 'HEART OF GOLD':

The horse stuff in that one was pretty cool, because we had saddle falls and horse falls. Saddle falls are where the rider will fall off the horse, and the horse fall is where the actual horse will go down as well. We had two or three of both of those in there, and then there was a hovercraft deal that had a big machine gun on on the back that was quite fun. There were a couple of different rigs. There was one where the hovercraft was actually towed behind another vehicle on a trailer [as seen on page 99], and the trailer was painted out to make it look like it was floating. Then there were pieces of it – there was another one that was on the soundstage that just kind of moved as if it was going over bumps and stuff with green screen in the back. There were a lot of people taking bullet hits, the one guy in the back of the hover vehicle took a nice hit coming off of that.

ON 'OBJECTS IN SPACE':

We had a sequence in that where Jubal Early [played by Richard Brooks] fights Mal in the confines of the ship itself. Obviously, for the moves in that, you're restricted to a lot of close combat kind of stuff, rather than nice big flashy jumping kicks, because there's no room. It can work in two ways. It can make the fight look more intense or it can limit you so much that it looks pretty boring, so you've got to try to use the space that you have in the best way you can.

IN CONCLUSION:

I think the whole concept was unique. I love the way that Joss developed it. I haven't talked to anybody who saw it that didn't like it. In terms of stunts, I think we were a very safe show. I had a great time filming it and we all got along very well. It was just a great series.

SEAN MAHER

Dr Simon Tam

SEAN ON THE WORLD OF THE SHOW, AND THE MOVIE:

What I love about the world of *Firefly* is it's 500 years in the future but there's this big 'what if?', like, what if we used up the resources of Earth and here we are, people are trying to survive, trying to get by, trying to just eat and get a job... For me it instilled this faith in humanity that, yes, 500 years in the future we have this Alliance trying to do this horrible thing to this girl and trying to change people, [but] at the end of the day it's like, "OK, let's just have faith." There is innate goodness, and people will prevail as human beings... there's just a wonderful sense of humanity to it. No matter how far in the future you go, hopefully people are people in how they work and function together. We are trying to rebuild and figure things out.

INTERVIEW WITH ZETAMINOR.COM, 2005

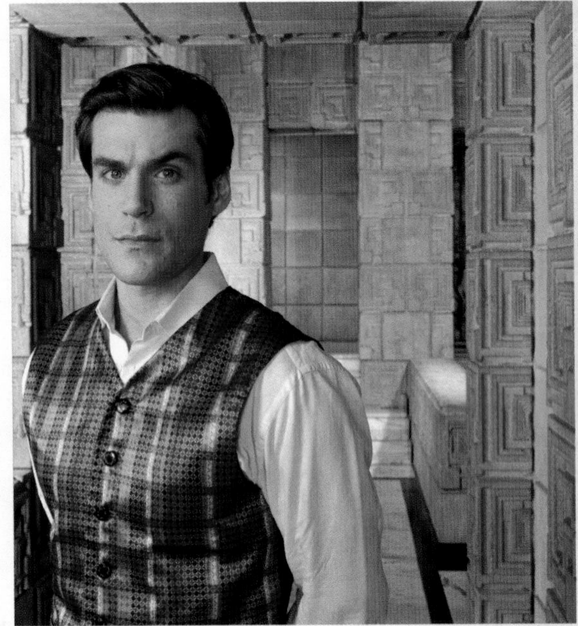

ON JOSS WHEDON:

He's just this incredible man, he's really a wonderful guy, a friend and a mentor. The instant I met him... I was so intrigued. I really wanted to work with him. And it just continually grew, like every time on set, watching him work, everything he said was so smart. I felt that I was being steered into the right direction. He's this incredible ring leader.

INTERVIEW WITH ZETAMINOR.COM, 2005

SEAN MAHER

ON THE FRUSTRATION OF BEING IN TV SHOWS THAT GOT CANCELED:

It got easier. I think the first time it happened, it was like a death. When *Ryan Caulfield* got canceled... Y'know, it was my first job, and you do kind of live in this bubble before you air. You think this show is the most amazing thing, and you're doing six, seven episodes before you go to air, so you've created bonds with people and you feel like a family. So *Ryan Caulfield* felt a bit like a death. And then, by the time I got to *Firefly*... The irony of the *Firefly* journey, for me, was that when it was canceled, I was like, "Oh well, chalk it up to another canceled show." And that was when Joss was like, "No way. We're not done. We're gonna make a movie." And I was like, "Yeah, right. I've heard this before." Because I felt like I had been jaded, because I think that was my... fourth canceled show. So,

yeah, by the time *Firefly* got canceled, I think I was a little used to it, and just felt like, "All right, well, let's move on to something else." So that's why I'm always so shocked at the *Firefly* phenomenon. It was the exact opposite of what I had been used to. Because when *Ryan Caulfield* was canceled, all those discussions were going on. "It's not done. We're going to a different network. We're doing this. We're doing that..." Like I even related that to my agent, "Oh no, this isn't finished. Don't you worry. We're going to find a home for this. That's what they're telling me on set. It's fine." And you know, it never happens, or rarely happens, I guess. *Firefly* is the little engine that could. It's a phenomenon of its own.

INTERVIEW WITH SEANMAHER.INFO, 2009

ON GETTING THE PHONE CALL ABOUT THE MOVIE:

I remember exactly where I was. I was on Orlando, it's a street in LA just north of Melrose, and I pulled off to the side of the road because I was just like, "Wait, what? We're really doing this?" And my agent was like, "We have the offer." And I was, "All right, I gotta go!" And then we [the cast] all called each other: "Did you get an offer?" [Laughs.] ... I honestly didn't believe that it was going to happen. Even at the read-through... We kept laughing because we couldn't believe we were doing this. I'd look over at Jewel and she'd be like, "Heeheehee!"

INTERVIEW WITH SEANMAHER.INFO, 2009

ON THE FANS:

It's just wonderful, it just brings you home. I mean, all the time, people... like the Immigrations Officer tonight [Sean had just flown into Vancouver when this interview took place] was all, this is business business, talk talk talk, and then as I'm walking away, he said, "*Firefly* rules." And I was like, "Thanks, buddy." They're everywhere, the fans... It's extraordinary to be part of something that reached so many people. And I feel like people continue [to find it]... People who have recently seen the show, new fans who are like, "Oh my gosh, my girlfriend made me watch it this weekend and I was so happy and what an amazing show!" I just feel like everybody who gets a taste of it, loves it. I'm always amazed at that. I feel like I've rarely met – or maybe people don't tell me – people who've seen the show, who didn't like it."

INTERVIEW WITH SEANMAHER.INFO, 2009

HIS FAVORITE MEMORY OF JOSS:

My favorite moment – and he wasn't on the set – but we were shooting the series and I remember the time when his first child was born. That sort of epitomizes to me how much of a family I feel with these people. To be on set and get word that Joss had his first child, and how moving that was."

INTERVIEW WITH ABOUT.COM, 2005

ON LOCATION

An interview with Location Manager Peter Robarts

While most of the interiors for *Firefly*, including the sets for the ship Serenity, existed on the soundstages of Twentieth Century Fox Studios in Los Angeles, when it came time to visit a planet, the cast and crew often headed off for a location shoot.

This is where *Firefly* location manager Peter M. Robarts came in. So what exactly does the job entail? Robarts explains: "A location manager reads the script, and all the different locations that are written in the storyline – whether it's a gas station, the beach, a building, a rooftop, a bar or whatever it is – a location manager needs to go out and find different options for each of them. Then he'll present them all to the director for him to choose which one he thinks is best for the show. And then a location manager has to arrange for all the city and county permits for filming in those locations, as well as arrange for all the physical choreography of getting a group of people into a location – parking lots for crew, places to park all the trucks – all that kind of stuff."

Robarts had been working for Mutant Enemy for over a year as location manager on *Buffy the Vampire Slayer* when *Firefly* came along. "A lot of the people went from *Buffy* to *Firefly* – I was one of those – to do the pilot and the series," Robarts notes. "The premise was a pretty interesting one. I love sci-fi, and it was also combined with a frontier setting, in which you went to these different planets and people rode horses and used guns — not ray guns. We weren't looking for a whole lot of hi-tech buildings and hi-tech exteriors. We kept it much more open, out in the frontier regions, where the Serenity crew were shipping their trade. A lot of the stuff that we in the location department were looking for were old abandoned towns, vacant valleys, a lot of mines and just interesting terrain that you'd probably shoot more in a Western than you would normally think of in sci-fi. We were looking for really interesting, otherworldly geography that could be on some other remote planet somewhere."

How does one find such locations? "If you've been in the business long enough," Robarts points out, "you know all these different places, because over the years, you've shot them from time to time on different shows. So most of the stuff that we shot, I knew all about from before."

Many of the desert 'Western' locations were several hours' drive out of Los Angeles. Why were such distant sites chosen? "Well, it just depends on what you're looking for," Robarts says. "If you want real desert, you've got to go out to Palmdale or Lancaster. Those are your closest ones. Also, you want to get away from a lot of houses. Every time you go out, every couple of months, there are more houses on your horizon, which is sort of what's happening to Los Angeles in a lot of ways. But the best deserts, you have to go out to that area, out toward Mojave. Not *to* Mojave, but on the way out to Mojave, which is where Lancaster and Palmdale are."

'SERENITY':

"In the pilot, they had a huge battle scene in Serenity Valley. That was a really interesting look that we needed to find, and we found it in a valley out toward the Mojave Desert, in the Palmdale/Lancaster area. There is this really terrific desert valley full of huge boulders and lots of sand, really nice and wide with a sort of desert bowl area off to one side of it. And it was quite large: hundreds of yards long and hundreds of yards wide, so it fit what we needed very well. There's another place that we shot the big scene with Patience and her gang, down in a big dry wash. That was a ranch out by Acton, by the 14 freeway."

❖ Opposite: Meeting Patience and her gang, out by Acton, CA.

❖ Above and top: Filming the battle of Serenity Valley.

❖ Above and right: The Tropico Gold Mine became Paradiso.

'THE TRAIN JOB':
"There was a high-speed train that came into an old desert town and a mine. That was out at Rosamond, just north of Lancaster, about two hours north of Los Angeles, and it's an old gold mine that sits on a hill. I think they went back there on the feature [*Serenity*]. That was an interesting location — the Tropico Gold Mine it's called."

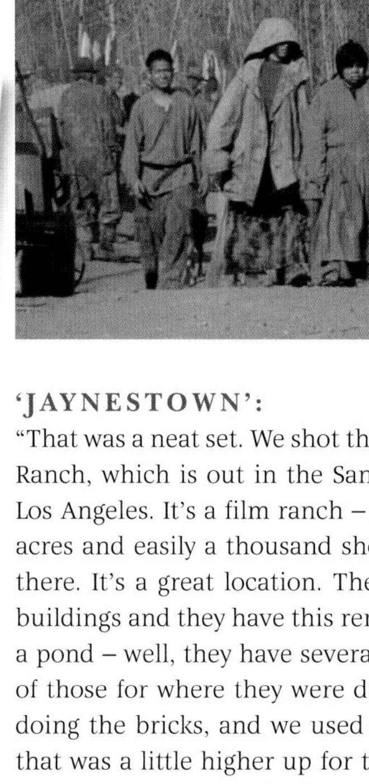

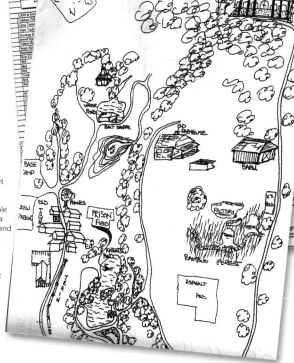

❖ Right: A callsheet for one of the days spent filming 'Jaynestown' at Sable Ranch, along with a map given to cast and crew to help orient them.

❖ Opposite left center and bottom: Sable Ranch as it is today.

'JAYNESTOWN':
"That was a neat set. We shot that at a place called Sable Ranch, which is out in the Santa Clarita area north of Los Angeles. It's a film ranch – it's about four hundred acres and easily a thousand shows have been shot out there. It's a great location. They have lots of different buildings and they have this remarkably large area with a pond – well, they have several, actually. We used one of those for where they were digging the mud out and doing the bricks, and we used one of the other ponds that was a little higher up for the prison where people were in cages over water."

'ARIEL':
"We were on the Fox lot, because it was a Fox show, so for a lot of the exteriors we needed we shot some of the nice modern buildings that they have there, in Century City."

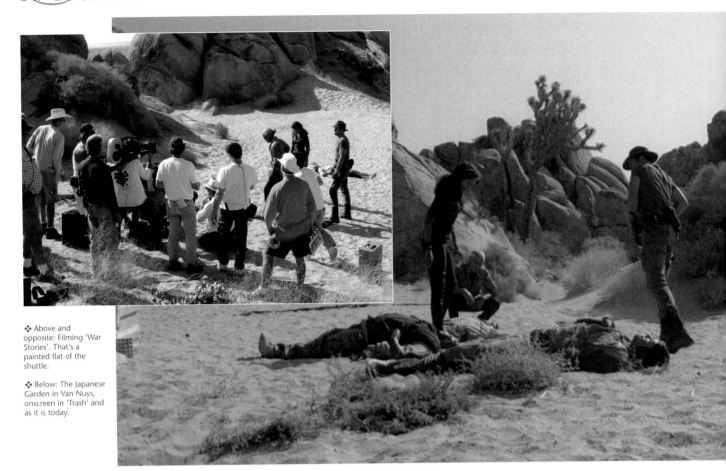

❖ Above and opposite: Filming 'War Stories'. That's a painted flat of the shuttle.

❖ Below: The Japanese Garden in Van Nuys, onscreen in 'Trash' and as it is today.

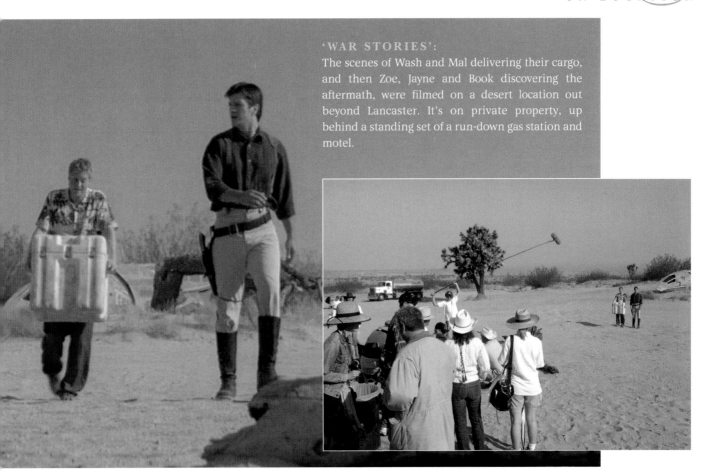

'WAR STORIES':
The scenes of Wash and Mal delivering their cargo, and then Zoe, Jayne and Book discovering the aftermath, were filmed on a desert location out beyond Lancaster. It's on private property, up behind a standing set of a run-down gas station and motel.

'TRASH':
Robarts did not work on the last two *Firefly* episodes to be filmed, 'Trash' and 'The Message'. "At that time," he says, "they weren't sure if they had been picked up to do a couple more episodes and I went off to do another show." The exteriors for Durran Haymer's estate on Bellerophon in 'Trash' were shot at the Japanese Garden in Van Nuys, California. The garden's Japanese name, Suiho-en, means "garden of water and fragrance", which is somewhat ironic given that it is right next to the Tillman Water Reclamation Plant, which treats sewage. However, the garden itself is a beautiful location, with migratory waterfowl, tilapia and carp inhabiting its ponds and a variety of traditional Japanese tea garden architecture and landscaping. The garden is open to the general public.

'HEART OF GOLD':

"That was a private compound that's way, way out past Lancaster. I'd heard about it, so I went out there and it was this two-story or two-and-a-half-story old mansion that some desert person had half-built. He'd built it on the inside, but a lot of the outside was left unfinished – actually, some of the inside, too – and there was all kinds of trash and everything all over the place. It was a bizarre but really unique location, and that's what we used for the ladies of ill repute. There was some kind of an airfield there, too, that he had outlined with tires. It was a very eclectic property, and it really fit what we were looking for on that particular show."

❖ Above: Prepping a shot for 'Heart of Gold'.

❖ Right: Filming the attack. The gunmen on the right are firing pellets to simulate bullet hits on the house.

❖ Far right: Adding some prop blood.

WHAT MIGHT HAVE BEEN:
Having used several places within striking distance of LA, Robarts looked further afield at Death Valley for possible future locations, though ultimately *Firefly* never filmed there. "I went for a big scout out there, thinking that we would be using a lot of that stuff. I'm sure that had we gone another season, if it had been picked up, we probably would have gone to a lot of really interesting areas out towards Death Valley, because there's some *really* otherworldly places out there, which would have been great to shoot." He's sorry it didn't last longer. "*Firefly* had a very interesting group of people, very talented. It was a fun shoot, and it was a great crew."

❖ Top right: The house encased in foil during filming, and (top left) as it is today.

❖ Above left: The hovercraft trailer rig.

❖ Left: Actor Fredric Lehne takes a test drive.

SUMMER GLAU

River Tam

SUMMER ON DEVELOPING HER ACTING SKILLS:

The thing about River that I like is that she doesn't have a lot of lines. Especially in the series she had to show what she was thinking just by the way she moved, or by how her face was moving. I think that has helped me a lot as an actor. I still have a hard time sometimes, expressing my anger with words, I'm better at moving and being in a room and showing how I feel that way. It's a thing that I had to work on because I was very shy as a kid. I think that's why I love dancing, because I felt that people were watching me but I didn't have to connect with them. They were out there and I could feel that they were watching me, but I didn't have to look at them. Now with acting it's very therapeutic for me, having to actually say and communicate.

INTERVIEW WITH ZETAMINOR.COM, 2005

ON JOSS WHEDON:

If you stand by him on set for ten minutes you realize every detail that runs by him, you realize how special, creative and patient he is. He is kind, and he speaks well to everybody. He gave me what I have now in my career, he cast me in my very first TV show, he believed in me when nobody believed in me. He saw something that other people were not seeing. He's my hero in a way. I'll never forget what he's done for me.

INTERVIEW WITH ZETAMINOR.COM, 2005

ON FILMING THE 'SESSION 416' VIRAL MARKETING CAMPAIGN FOR THE MOVIE:

It was very exciting for me to be involved in that. I was in Texas... Joss called me and said, "Where are you? Can you come back for the weekend? I have this idea but I need to write it!" I was thrilled and I felt it was really important for people to see River before anything happened to her, when she was happy and full of hope.

I loved doing it. It was just Joss and me and it's a really special memory for me. I thought the script was very haunting. I remember when I was trying to memorize it, I hadn't been in my LA apartment for a month. I was lying in bed trying to memorize the dialogue that I was going to shoot the next morning. I couldn't sleep that night going in and out of bad dreams and talking to myself. I got scared from trying to prepare for those emotional scenes. It was a hard night to get through, the words were powerful.

INTERVIEW WITH SUMMERGLAU.CO.UK, 2005

JEWEL STAITE ON MEETING SUMMER FOR THE FIRST TIME:

Jewel: [Summer was] very quiet and shy and beautiful and fairy-like. Very elegant in her posture – you could tell she was a dancer. We were all at the read-through and you opened your mouth and you gave this crazy-ass performance out of nowhere. At read-throughs you sort of give it fifty percent, and Summer gave it like 100 percent and I was like, "Oh my god!" She just floored me; I just couldn't believe how good she was, and how perfect she was for the role.

Summer: I get really sappy when I talk about everyone. I was the new kid and I'd never done anything before and

SUMMER GLAU

TO REMOVE
FWD
AFT
LUMBAR
LOCK

when Jewel said that we were at the table read and I was reading full out — I didn't *know* that we were supposed to read through the script, I thought that we had to perform at the table. I finally grew into learning how to be an actor... I love everybody, I really do. I admire everyone.

SPEAKING ON STAGE AT THE 'SERENITY' CONVENTION, 2005

ON WHERE RIVER, WHO ARRIVED ON THE SHIP NAKED, GOT HER CLOTHES FROM:

I think River collected clothes from Kaylee and Inara, and also there were a few dresses that we made up a little backstory for ourselves that Simon would pick them up from stops along the way. Like the pink dress that I wore in 'The Message', which was my favorite actually. It was an old vintage dress from the forties. We just figured that one day Simon was out shopping and he saw it and picked it up because he thought River would like it. I loved my wardrobe. I thought it was the most comfortable out of anybody's. So I think she just picked up little scraps and wore strange little things, whatever might fit on her, and I think she raided Inara's closet and Kaylee's too.

SPEAKING ON STAGE AT THE 'FUSION' CONVENTION, 2004

ON HER CHARACTER'S 'DEFINING MOMENT':

I think that one of the favorite scenes I ever did was in 'Objects in Space' after I had been up in Jubal Early's ship. The crew had been trying to get rid of me for so many episodes and when Mal comes up onto the ship to bring me back, that's one of my favorite moments. I felt like they were really my family and that they were going to take care of me, and that I was accepted. I think that was an important moment for my character, and a scene that I really love.

SPEAKING ON STAGE AT THE 'FUSION' CONVENTION, 2004

CRYSTAL

// BY BRETT MATTHEWS

Simon looked...

It was hard to find the word. He wasn't helping, not offering anything beyond the gentle smile he had not worn sincerely in too long. He looked at her directly, but it wasn't a stare. Didn't make her uncomfortable in the smallest way.

The word came suddenly, as obvious and clear to her as it had been elusive only moments before.

Simon Tam was happy. They were finally safe.

"River."

Simon's face resolved slowly, lines drawing out of thin air to form it. His brow was furrowed. He was no longer happy. He stared at River, more as a clinician than her brother, which *always* made her uncomfortable.

"How do you feel?"

She could see the hypo he had used to inject her sitting on a surface in the infirmary. River had come to hate the place and its cold, even light. She didn't say anything for a while. She wasn't sure of the answer. She watched as Simon continued to sharpen, to the point she felt she could count all the pores of his face.

"*River.*" More urgently this time. It had been

about a minute.

It made River lose count, somewhere in the hundreds. She brought her eyes to Simon, slow and steady and sure. He flinched as if he didn't recognize her... or as though he *did*. Like when you see someone you haven't for a very long time.

"*Crystal.*" That was the word. And with it River Tam was off, wandering Serenity's twisting corridors. She hoped as she had so many times before...

Simon let her go. As always, he would not be far behind.

It's hard to describe what River saw next.

Bodies. Limbs. Tongues. Writhing like oiled snakes. She could all but feel their slickness on the surface of her skin...

And the *sounds*. Pleasure or pain. Maybe even both.

"Why you lookin' at me like that, Moon Pie?"

Jayne was in the kitchen area. He brought a steaming pot of soy-something over to the large, wooden surface where River sat. The table had enough room for all of them, but it occurred to her that soon, they'd start removing chairs. In this moment, River felt she could divine exactly how and when the seats would turn up empty.

No. She *knew* it...

"What's the matter? You gone deaf on top of *dinlo*?"

He had used the masculine form — as Jayne often did, overcompensating — but the translation was one of River's very favorites. *Dinlo*. Crazy. But it was the literal that she loved. *Electric man.*

"I reckon this stuff would taste just as good coming out the other end..." Jayne mumbled as he took a seat across from her, at the spot he'd carved his name, long ago. He'd etched other expressions into the table, too. None for polite company. Marking his territory from the moment he had decided to stay aboard the ship. When he grudgingly realized, though he would never admit it, that the lot of everyone aboard and Jayne Cobb's were one and the same.

His knife speared a block of purple tofu, worked it around the stump of tobacco clenched in his teeth and into his mouth. Jayne's face twisted, not much different from the times he'd been shot.

"I were runnin' this boat, it'd be strawberries and salmon. *Guaranteed.*"

The sound of his eating jogged her to what she'd just seen and heard so clearly, no matter that it was the future. River's stomach turned despite being empty. Maybe that was why the mixture of drugs Simon had injected her with was having such a profound effect. He had told her to eat before her treatment. She should have listened.

"You'll never captain your own ship, but it's going to be fine. You'll be happy as you define it. Even heroic, from time to time."

River swept out of the dining room before Jayne could get the mouthful down. He had no idea what any of it meant. Maybe time would tell. He was not blind to the fact that it often did, where River was concerned.

"*Dinlo.*" Jayne said it again. That was a hell of a lot easier to deal with than the alternative...

"You die, Shepherd."

Book didn't so much as blink.

"We all die, child. It's merely a question of when. And more importantly, for what." His answer reassured River. His answers often did.

"Yes. But you die first."

He blinked, that time. But Book was immediately at peace.

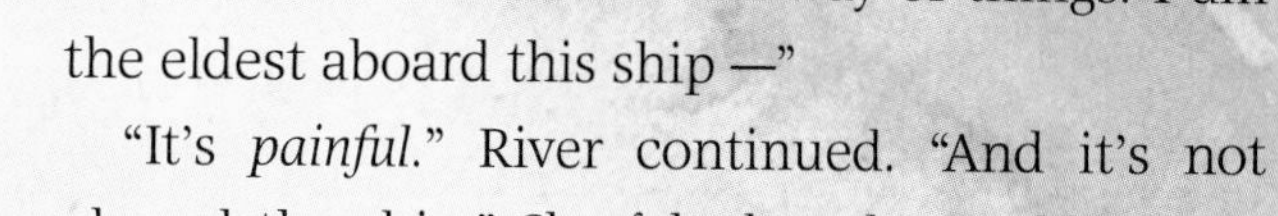

"Seems to me the normal way of things. I am the eldest aboard this ship —"

"It's *painful.*" River continued. "And it's not aboard the ship." She felt that she could talk to him, at once more easily and directly than anyone else. "Do you want to know how it happens? Do you want to know where?"

Book fingered the braided locks of his hair, didn't notice it made her fear they might pop loose. Of the questions that occurred to him since River had broken the silence of his morning prayers, neither of the two she had asked.

"No. What I would want to know is this. Am I alone? Is it for something I believe is *right...?*"

River relaxed profoundly. Those were so much easier to answer than her own. She knew them innately, as an infant knows to draw its first breath. Took air herself, preparing to share what she had seen — was it *experienced*? — with the Shepherd. She would have told him anything he asked. Anything in her power, which on this day, this hour, seemed limitless...

"On second thought," Book spoke before River had the chance. "I'd prefer not knowing." He smiled, broad and brilliant and white.

"I've chased mysteries my whole life, divine and otherwise. I see no point in stopping now."

"Ain't interrupting, River. Doing the count's easy, you can count all that we got on one hand."

She had found Zoe in the cargo bay, taking inventory of their supplies. But River didn't come any further down the suspended catwalk than she already was.

"You're going to be okay," she said from the

"It looks like a pig."

Of this River was certain.

Kaylee squirmed in her hammock to clock where she stood, at the threshold of the engine room. River spun a finger in a circle, pantomiming the action of Serenity's cabled heart, revolving around its spit of a piston.

Kaylee took it as a compliment of the highest order. Impossibly, her face brightened even more.

"Pigs is yummy!"

She motioned that River should join her in the hammock, an image Jayne would have deemed *bunk-worthy*. River shook her head.

"I can't stay. It's running out. But I wanted to thank you..." Her voice was serene. If Kaylee wasn't looking at River as she spoke, she might not have recognized it at all.

shadows above.

It didn't come as any surprise to Zoe, not even enough to warrant looking up from the work. For her, there simply was no other option.

"'Course we are. We've been without before, will be again." She scratched four lines with lead into a piece of brown paper as she spoke. There wasn't enough stock to warrant a fifth, the slash that should have gone through them. "Not that I'd mind having to carry a one, from time to time."

"It will seem impossible. It's almost going to break you. In the small hours, when no one is around..."

Now Zoe's head snapped up. River met her gaze and held it, not something that happened to Zoe often.

"But you're going to be okay."

Zoe nodded almost imperceptibly and River took a step back, disappearing into the darkness. She'd said what she came to and she'd been heard. That was about as much as anyone could ever ask of words.

Zoe started the count over.

"Thank me? Whatever for?"

"Long story." River smiled. "*Beautiful* story." Then she was simply gone.

"You're welcome!" Kaylee's voice echoed down the hall, bouncing around its slanted shape. She sighed and swung herself out of the rope's embrace, yellowed picture novels and technical manuals spilling out along with her, equal in her eyes as pleasure reading. In the former, the boy and girl often ended up together. Or failing that, died wonderfully in the pursuit. But the latter had *schematics*. Annotations on hydraulics and fluid mechanics. And gobs of other things, even if they were wrong sometimes or Kaylee knew from experience the method they advised could be done twenty-five to fifty percent better.

She sighed again, plucking her favorite socket wrench off a loop of her coveralls and approaching the engine, which had begun to emit a funny sound.

Kaywinnit Lee Frye had a pig to attend to.

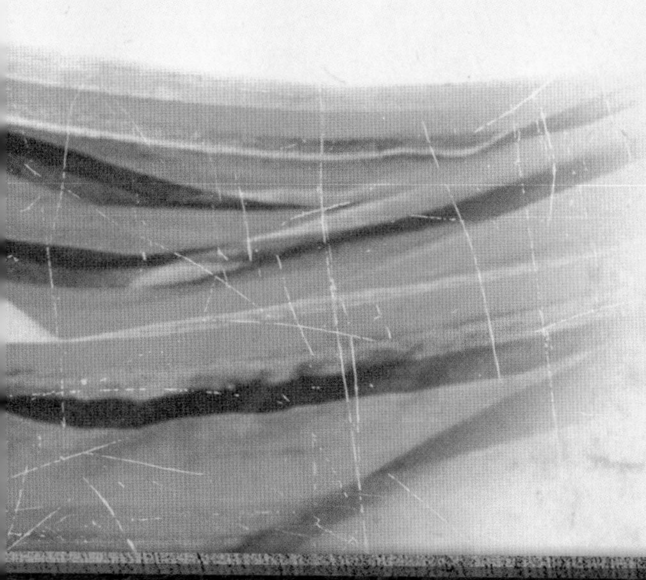

Wash looked over the flight yoke, into the familiar black of space. The dash was void of dinosaurs, making it easy. You put dinosaurs up there — *one time* — and it was all anyone wanted to talk about. It was much the same with flowered shirts...

He felt River's presence and spun the jump seat around to greet her. Wash got used to people coming up behind him, working in a cockpit. And though he couldn't always tell who was there so instantly, apart from his wife, there was never any mistaking River. She radiated something no one else aboard the ship — that Wash had ever known, for that matter — put out. She *crackled*.

"Howdy, Sunshine. Come to keep a pilot company while we limp to the cheapest fuel deck?"

River stepped into the light of the instrument panels. Her appearance concerned him. It looked to Wash like she was going to cry.

"River. What's the matter? Has Jayne been telling you where babies come from again...?"

She continued forward, throwing her arms around Wash and embracing him. *Urgently.* So tight the air was squeezed from his lungs and his question trailed off, unanswered. River was stronger than she looked. Stronger than anyone knew...

She released him just as suddenly. Her hand was last to break contact, fingertips describing an erratic shape around the whole of his chest, like a heart but larger and lopsided. Finally withdrew reluctantly. River spun on her bare heel and left the cockpit without crying, or even saying a word.

"*Right.* Because that happens every day. Is there some obscure holiday I don't know about —"

"You know what would happen, I found you huggin' on some sweet young thing, wasn't

certifiable?" River and Zoe had crossed paths, again in the hall.

"You'd murder me?" Wash opened his arms the familiar, perfect amount.

"No." Zoe said. "Most places, murder requires them finding the body."

She kicked the door shut and lowered herself into his lap.

"We got anything in our path?"

Wash shook his head.

"No ma'am. Nothing but empty space the next eight or so hours."

They kissed. It was exactly the right answer.

"Ask me."

River had entered the shuttle unannounced. Inara ended the conversation she was having over the Cortex immediately, somehow gracefully. Her potential client was not offended when the wave was cut short, instead even more intrigued.

"River –"

"*Ask me.*" It was more demand than question, this time.

Inara took River's hand and led her to the bed, piled high with fabrics from a dozen different worlds. She was cold to the touch, sweating hail.

"Ask you what?"

"What you *want.*" Her teeth were chattering, now. "Ask me and I'll tell you."

The way River said it made Inara believe her. She was more open-minded than most, given her profession as a Companion. Was not one to hold a grudge against things that were not easily explained.

"Running out of time..."

Two questions formed in Inara's mind at once, so distinctly they had faces. One was her own. The other familiar and handsome, if very stubborn. It occurred to her if she could only ask one, she didn't know which she would choose...

And then the faces were gone, replaced by River's. River was Inara's concern, not matters she had been too afraid to address with anyone — herself included — in far too long.

"Stay here. I'm going to find Simon."

"Yes and no." Inara was at the door when she heard them. The answers to her questions, but in which order? One would happen. The other would not. The revelation brought relief, maybe even joy...

But only for a moment. The other possibility soon seeped in, became every bit as palpable. Regret and despair.

Inara turned back to say something, just in time to see River hit the floor.

Malcolm Reynolds was dead.

He forced himself out of his bunk just the

same, pulled a coarse woolen shirt over too many scars and hitched up his suspenders. No shower today. Not out of preference, but because they hadn't been able to fill the reservoir before pushing off the latest rock that had offered them a job. Mal didn't even remember the planet's name at the moment, only that it was overly self-important in retrospect. He supposed people might say the same about the one he had chosen for his ship...

"*Serenity*." Mal whispered it to himself as she sailed as silently as she ever did through the black. He touched her rusted hull, could feel her pulse as surely as his own.

People might say that. But they'd be wrong.

He'd been up all night — it was *always* night in space — reaching out. Sending out feelers to various contacts, trying to find where the next tank of fuel or table of food might come from. Nothing so far, but it didn't worry Mal. His employers weren't the type to keep regular business hours.

Six of them, he figured, between now and when they'd be refueling. Plenty of time to suss how he was to pay for it. Something would come up. It always did. And if not, then Mal would have to make it...

Mal started up the ladder that led out of his quarters. The hatch atop popped open and he was in the hallway, which ran from stem to stern. And right on time, apparently. He stepped aside, letting the crush of crew and passengers pass.

"We didn't get paid, as you well know. So's I don't see the need for a parade —"

The sentence died on his lips the moment he saw they were carrying River.

Black. Stretching out indefinitely, without beginning or end...

It took River a moment to realize that it was space. The understanding allowed her to resolve the pinpricks of light that were very distant stars. So far away that were she to set course for them, she would not reach them in her lifetime. Not in ten.

The ship thrummed beneath her feet. Up the flight yoke and into the tips of her fingers, reverberating down the length of her arms and into her core. Her heart. Serenity's vibration was a promise between lovers, yearning to be fulfilled.

Of power just waiting to be unleashed...

River knew exactly how she — *the ship* — felt.

She reached up, flipping switches on and cutting others off, knowing where each was and what it did without looking. She increased the engine's gain and allowed Serenity to accumulate speed... not as much as either of them wanted, but River knew firsthand that a little bit of what you desired was often better than the whole.

River looked left to the co-pilot's seat, found Mal. Did he seem older? *Was* he older? It was hard to say. Malcolm Reynolds had a timeless quality about him she had always found comforting, that was constant and never went out of style. His expression asked the question for him, as it often did. *"We in a hurry or something?"* She smiled and answered aloud, though he had never spoke:

"No, Captain. We're just getting where we're going."

Mal was the first thing River saw when she awoke. He *had* looked older, just before.

It was the final moment of clarity before the fog set in, so fast and so thick it was soon raining in her head, making a mess of all that had come previously. River Tam began to... *wonder* about things. Large and small, consequential and not, all at once. Wonder wasn't the right word, but it was now as close as she could come.

More faces beyond Mal, all of them staring holes into her. River could feel the sear on her skin. All but smell her own flesh, going up...

River screamed and Mal smiled.

"There's our girl."

Jayne turned on the thick sole of his boot, stalking out of the infirmary.

"Seems fine to me, Doc. When do we eat?"

Simon watched River, considering...

River found Mal in the sunken area beneath the cockpit. It didn't have a name, really. There was never much reason to be there, beyond the occasional electrical issue and that it afforded perhaps the best view on the ship. This was as far

forward as one could get, just a sliver of transparent canopy between you and the cold crush of space...

Mal sometimes took his coffee there, as he did now. He looked up from the rim of his battered tin cup as River descended the ladder with a dancer's grace to join him.

"Sorry. Wanted to find you before. Ran out of time." She reached the deck. Mal kicked a stool over and River joined him, the two of them sitting before the quiet glory of the 'verse in mismatched chairs.

"Well, you found me now," Mal replied. "What was it you need?"

River craned her neck, listening to a song that only she could hear. Tried to filter its noise, to settle on the one frequency amidst thousands that would provide the answer... couldn't. The best she could do was:

"*This.* I don't know, but I think it was this."

Mal raised his cup. It was enough for him.

"Don't worry, sailor. It'll come to you. We've got all the time in the world..."

River looked out through the viewport as he did, hoping it were true. Even if she'd known, just hours before and with crystal clarity, that it wasn't.

"Sad, simple Simon..."

He looked down at River where she laid tucked in bed. Her eyes were heavy. Her cadence once again her own, more accurately that which had been imposed upon her. Scored into her brain with electrode-laced needles.

"I'm not sad, River. I'd like to think simple." Simon meant the words. He smiled as proof.

"Thought you fixed broken me." She yawned it out, was fading fast.

River was right. Neurologically, she was never closer to what she'd been before her abduction than today. And yet she was wrong, too.

"You're fine." Simon meant it every bit as much. "You're happier now than you were this morning. That means more to me than any readout from a machine."

Jayne's diagnosis — the irony of those two words paired was not lost on Simon — had been correct. River was undeniably different, now. And yet, in her own particular way, she was also right as rain. While Simon Tam would never abandon the search for the sister he knew, that he had helped raise and loved more than anything on any world he would ever visit, the events of the day had made him come to realize that he loved River — as she was now, falling asleep in front of him — every bit as much.

"You're fine." He said it again as he leaned low, kissing her forehead. Then Simon shut off the lights and slipped out of the berth.

And for one night, River slept without the interruption of dreams.

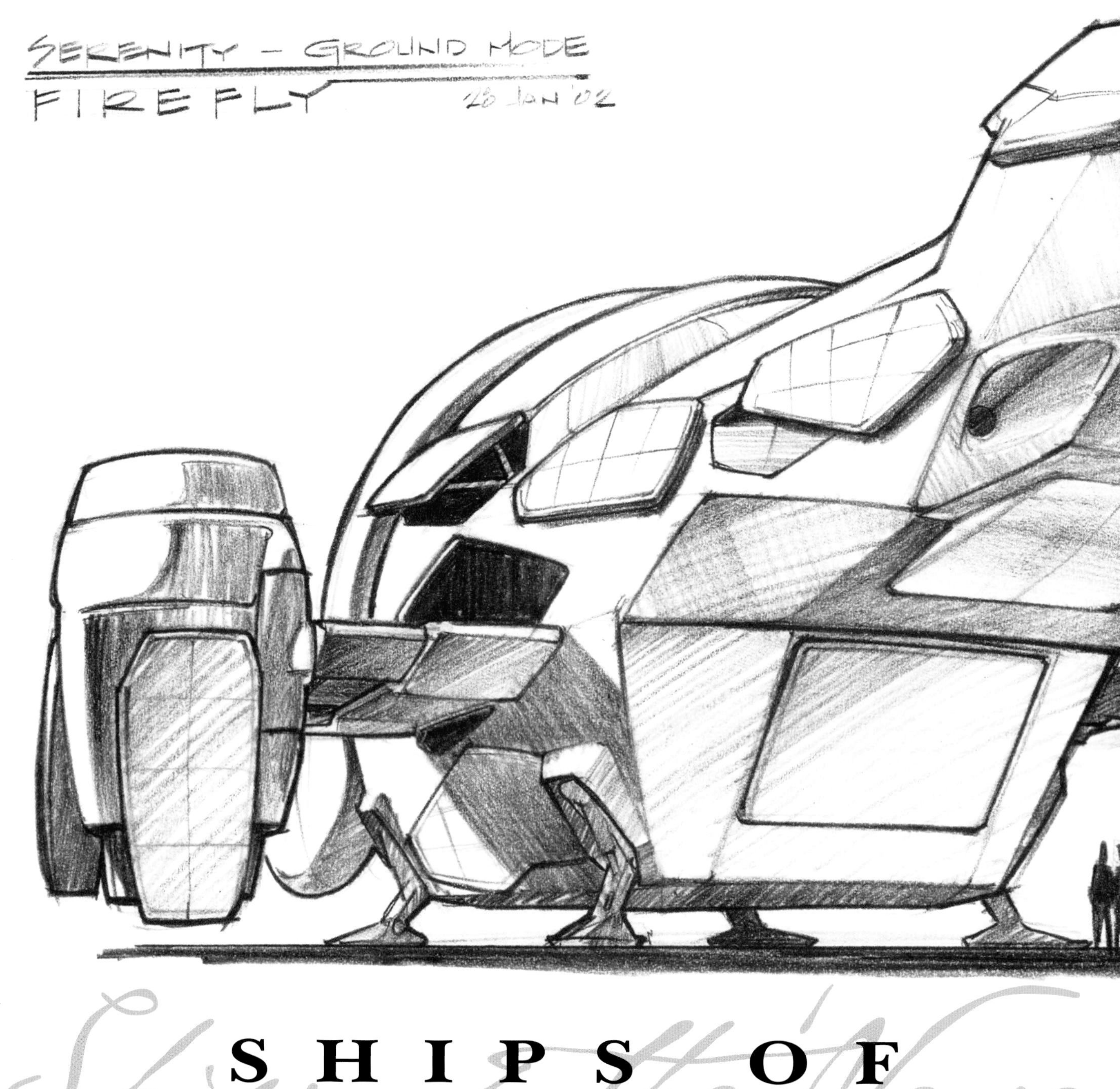

SHIPS OF THE 'VERSE

Designing the ships of Firefly

If Whedon was the master of the mythology and stories behind *Firefly*, then it was production designer Carey Meyer and visual effects supervisor/co-creator of Zoic Studios Loni Peristere who were the visual magicians, overseeing the design of all of the brilliant ships, vehicles and space stations that are now synonymous with the series. The two sat down together to reminisce about how they came to create the myriad of vehicles that were such an integral part of the show.

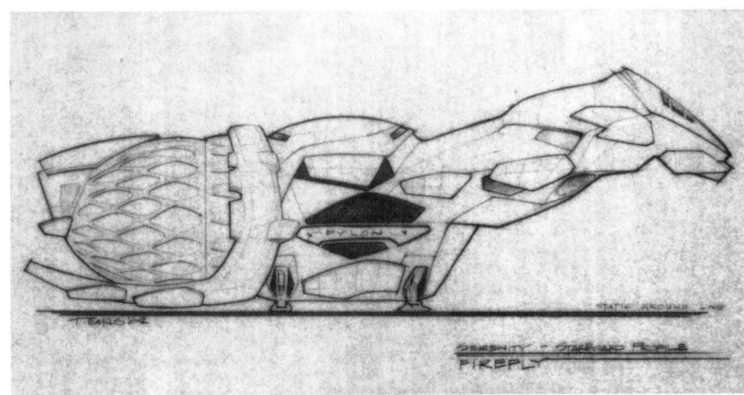

SERENITY

First and foremost let's make it clear – there really is no *Firefly* series without the Firefly class transport Serenity. In fact the ship was so important to Whedon, he told Meyer and Peristere that it was to be considered a character equal in standing to the cast. That mandate set the tone for how they approached its creation.

Meyer remembers, "When we were first starting the project, Joss was just getting the green light from Fox and we were all working on *Buffy* at the time. After a couple of weeks Joss came up to me and said he really wanted me to work on it and to pitch some ideas for what the ship would look like, because that was the starting point for him. Once he got an idea of what the world was like inside the ship, he could start formulating the stories. Joss said his one key was for it to have an ironic flair to it. It had to be cool, but there had to be some reality to it. So I started playing around with paper airplanes. There was this cool design I had always played around with as a child, and always loved. It's this conical-shaped airplane all made out of paper and I shoved a balloon into it.

"I still have the original model that I built," he chuckles. "I was up for 24 hours building this thing. We came in the next morning at nine o'clock and I think I nailed it. I brought the plane with the balloon shoved into it and a little sketch of what I was thinking. We all sit down and Joss says, 'Well, it's cool, but I think it's too far. We need to bring it back a little bit.' The shape was very asymmetrical, and he wanted a sleeker line to it. I took that original model and spread clay all over it, smoothing out the original into something resembling

❖ Opposite and above: Designs by illustrator Tim Earls helped refine Carey Meyer's original concept for Serenity.

what we have today. Then he really fell in love with what we now know as the ring that wraps around the rear."

Meyer continues, "From that point it was a series of sketches for how the rest of it all would look. He wanted a lot of it to look like an insect — a firefly obviously. One of the main designers I was looking at was Lebbeus Woods, who is a futurist architect. Joss liked that look as well, so we started sketching in that style, which got us an overall shape that we were able to cross-section and start developing the interior. From that Joss was able to ask for a bridge and a hallway that leads to the corridors, a galley, a corridor to the engine room and the main cargo bay. Once he nailed down the different spaces that were inside, we were able to lay it all out as set designs and work it back into the exterior shape."

Meanwhile Peristere says he was working in concert with Meyer in the digital realm. "I was keying off of what Carey was doing," he explains. "I began to build a temporary version of that ship in 3-D, so once we had a physical model we could immediately bring it into 3-D space. A lot of what we were doing was coming up with how the rooms fit, and fitting that into the 3-D model, adjusting so all the rooms would fit in a logical manner. And Carey had this cool idea that the ship was put together and then reconstructed a little bit, because it had been in a junkyard for a long time. So the idea was that the external panels weren't all original. We spent some time going in the direction of having a lot of variety of textures, with a lot of colors and patinas from other ships. We went too far at first because it was like a quilt of a spaceship, but we pulled back and streamlined it. We also took a look at the logistics of the neck of the ship, and played with how steep it was, and how close to the ground based on how you would drive stuff into the cargo bay when the landing gear was down. Then we had to come up with the right kind of landing gear, and the door/ramp into the cargo bay."

❖ Right and far right: More designs by Tim Earls.

❖ Below: Carey Meyer's early concept design for the ship.

❖ Opposite: Serenity, seen both as Zoic's CG model (above) and the sets, including the exterior of the shuttle cockpit set (center row, left).

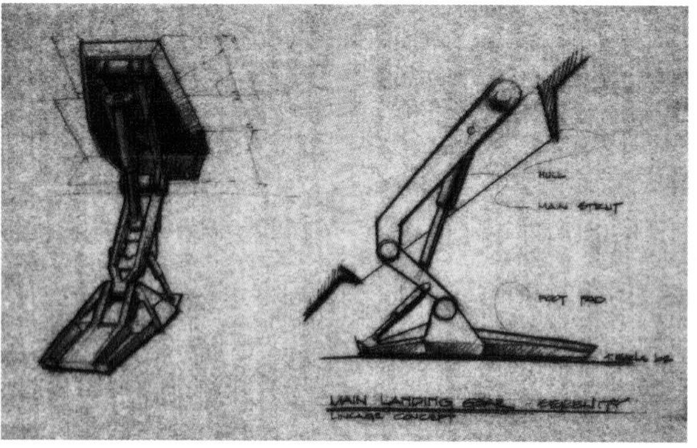

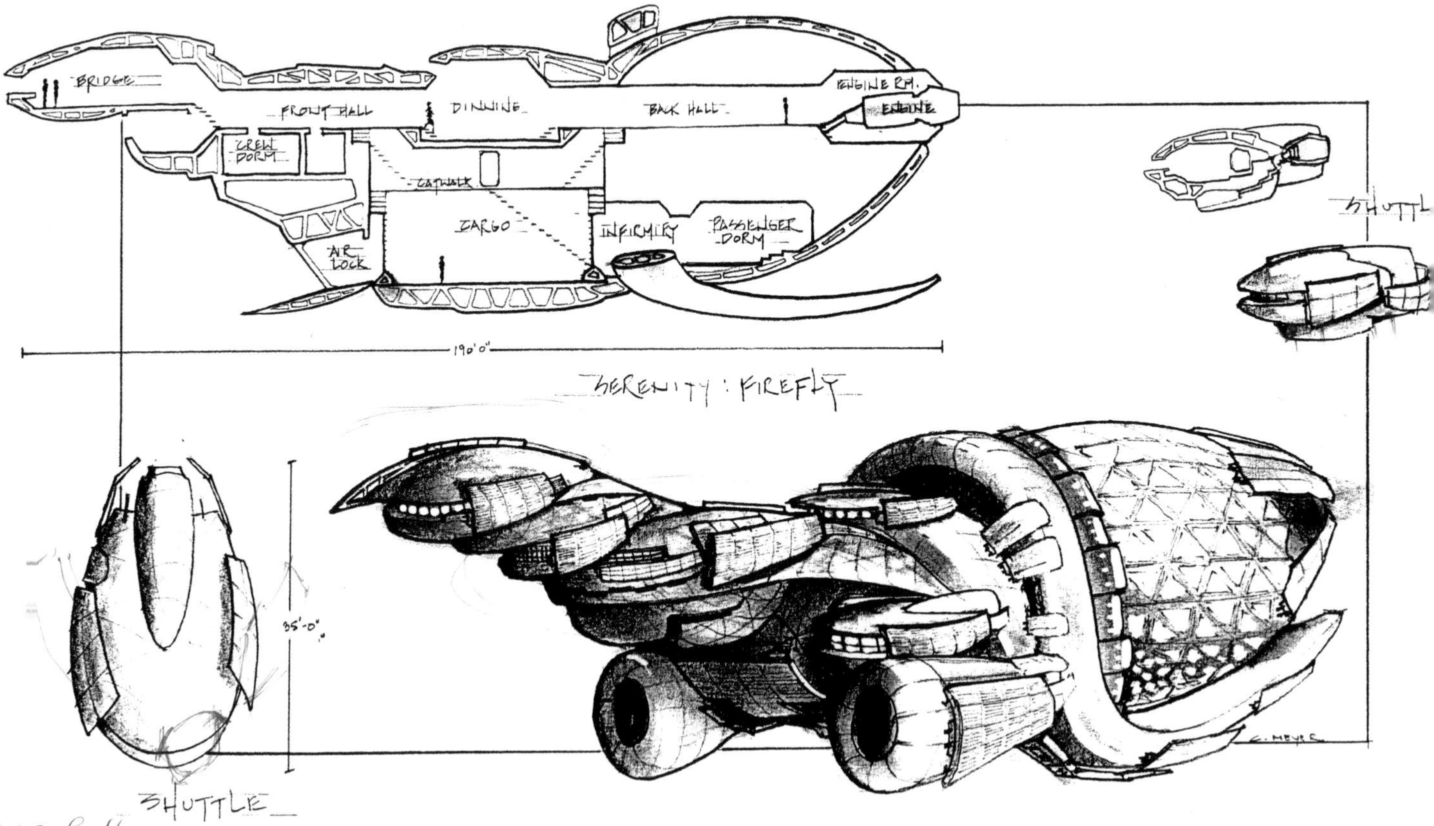

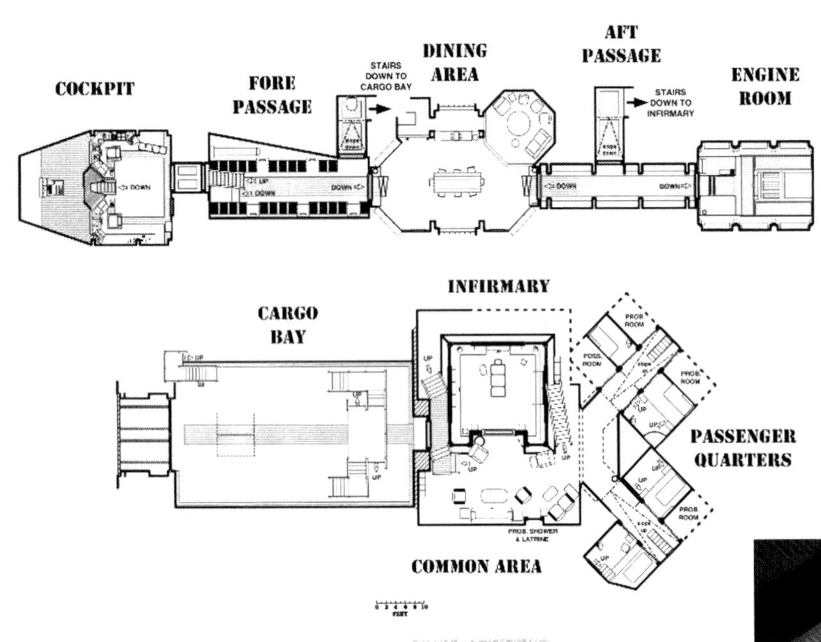

He continues, "In addition, we came up with where the gravity on the ship came from – we used the ring that Carey created. We called it the 'gravity ring' and put a widget in there that spun around. We built lighting effects for it with our DP on set, so they were built into the set lighting so you could see the changing flicker. We also had to come up with the trans-warp drive, the 'firefly engine'. Carey built these honeycomb shapes on the inside set, so we mirrored that on the outside. We came up with the logic of a cooling process, so we created these panels on the butt of the ship that opened up to reveal the same honeycomb pattern you saw on the inside, on the outside. There were insect-like panels that would show this glowing butt on Serenity, which was kinda cool."

SHUTTLE

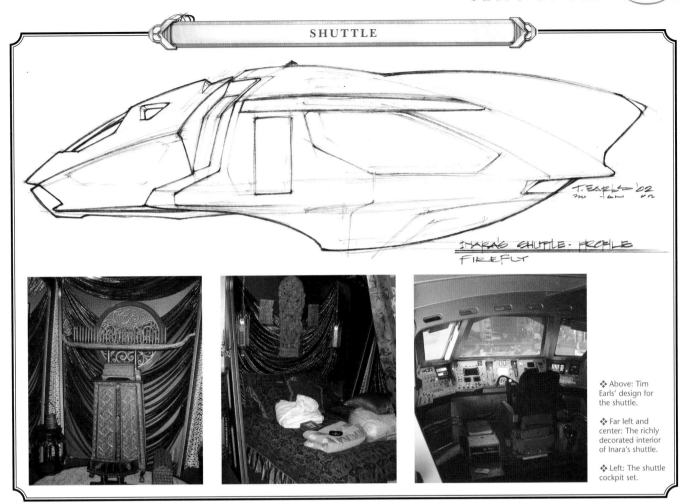

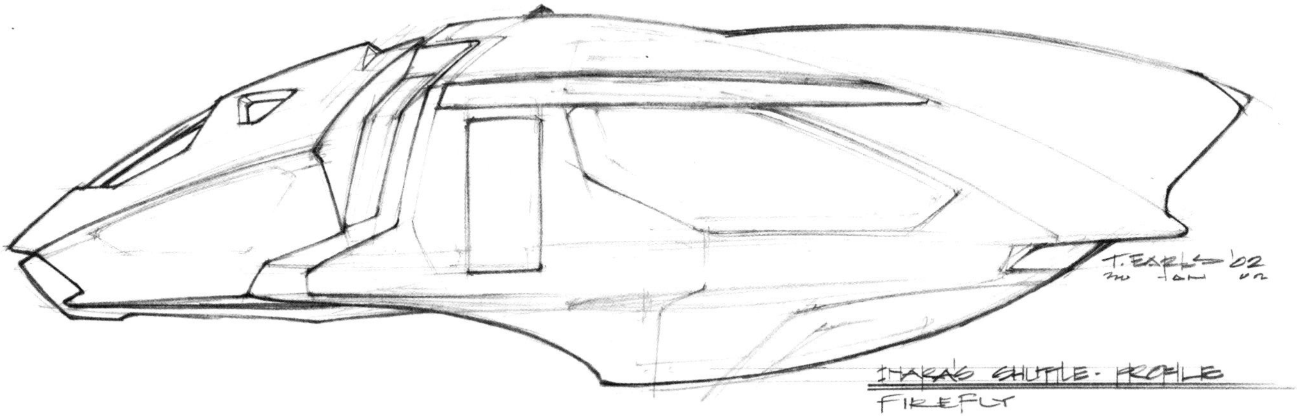

❖ Above: Tim Earls' design for the shuttle.

❖ Far left and center: The richly decorated interior of Inara's shuttle.

❖ Left: The shuttle cockpit set.

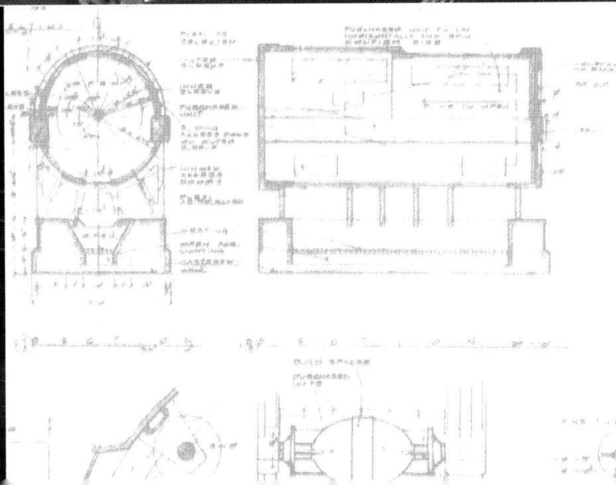

❖ Opposite center: A plan of the Serenity interior sets, showing how the various areas were actually joined together.

❖ Opposite, left and above: The bridge, interior corridors and original set blueprints.

Peristere laughs as he reveals an insiders' joke: "I always wanted Serenity's cargo bay to be detachable. Carey thought it was cool, but Joss was worried it was too similar to something that happened in *Star Trek*. I always thought a cargo ship's hold should be like a shipping container, where you can drop one off and pick one up. Believe it or not, I actually built it into the design of the CG model so that it does do that, because I figured at some time I would win that argument. I never won that fight, but it's still there."

Of their final product, Meyer muses, "Joss didn't just want a ship, he wanted a tenth character. I think we pulled it off and to this day he's very emotionally tied to that vehicle."

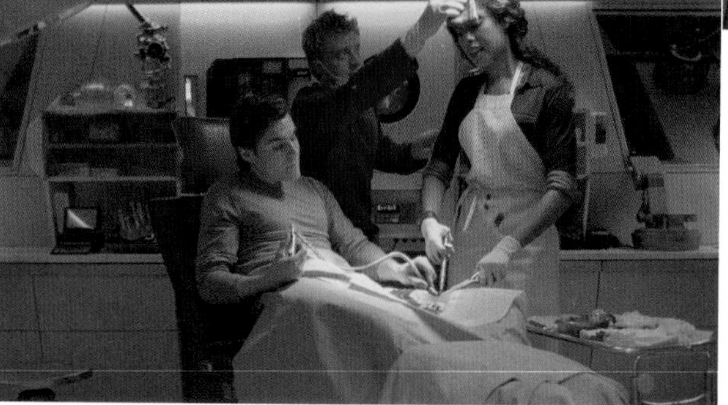

❖ Above: A bulkhead doorway, from blueprint to final set piece.

❖ Right: The infirmary.

❖ Below: The galley.

CONTROL PANEL SCREENS

❖ Top: A selection of control panel displays, which were printed onto transparencies and backlit.

❖ Above: The engine room.

❖ Above left and left: The cargo bay.

ALLIANCE CRUISER

These massive ships serve as functional cities that house military, police and civilians, patrolling the space between Alliance planets. After designing Serenity, Meyer says these were the next ships they tackled.

"We immediately knew we needed the Alliance ship and that it was a big craft – a sort of cityscape concept on a wing," Meyer details. "Joss was pretty clear right away that he didn't want to make something super long like the *Star Wars* Destroyer. He wanted it to be vertical... since it can go through space it doesn't have to worry about atmosphere. It can move whatever shape it is, so we started playing with it being tall. We did rough concept illustrations then sat down with illustrator Tim Earls and started creating."

Peristere continues, "The whole concept of a city in space was interesting to me. I love the notion of revealing a ship in an entirely new way, and one which embraced the fact that in space there is no up, down, right or left. There are no hard and fast rules of what you are looking at. I love how we introduce I.A.V. Dortmunder seeing two towers, thinking they are just great shapes, but then we reveal they are essentially Empire State buildings – these massive things! I love the idea that the tiny fighter craft show just how big this thing is. There's no need for scale in space – you can build ships as big as you like – so the idea of having this giant thing moving through the black was really cool. I was actually disappointed we didn't use the ship more, because we spent a lot of time working out the design of all of it, like the interesting bays on the underside where the fighter craft were stationed."

Carey adds, "The other concept we were playing with was that the textures and colors were completely divergent. The Alliance ship was stark grey with blacks and whites, while Serenity was very warm and had texture and felt real."

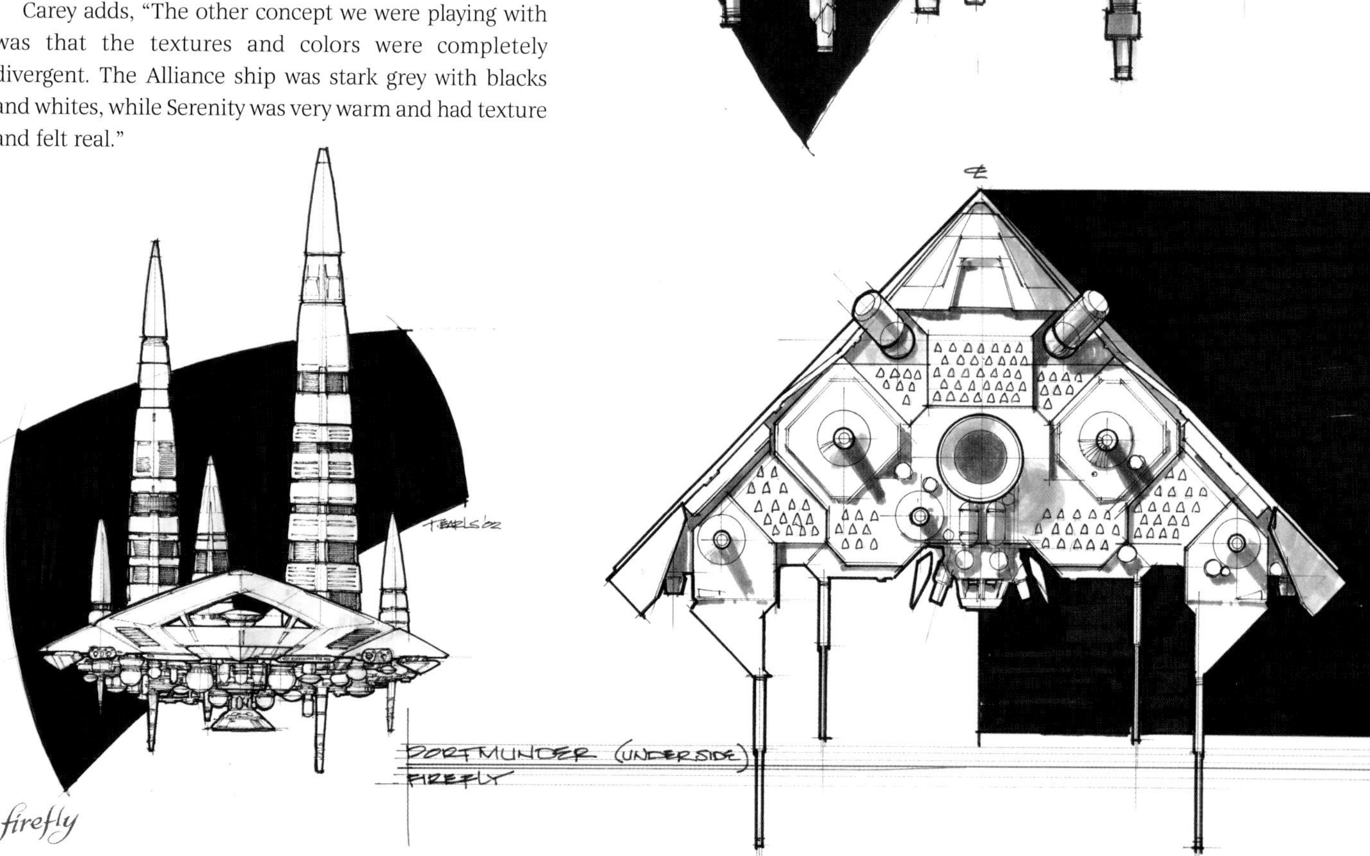

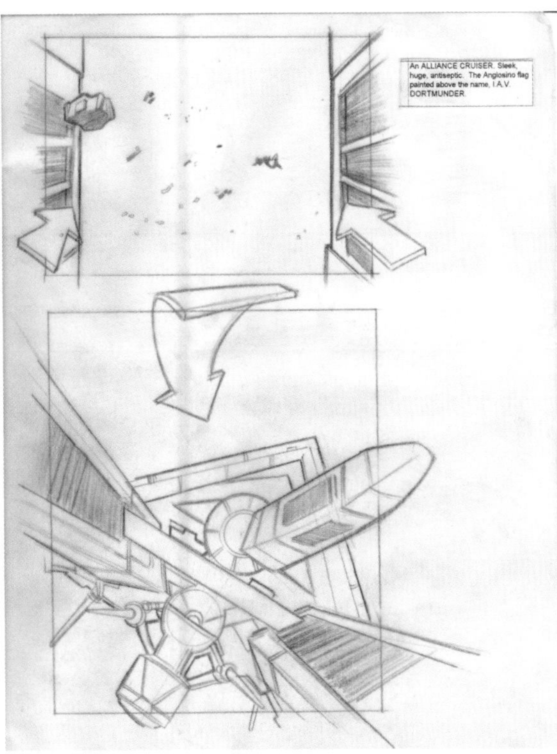

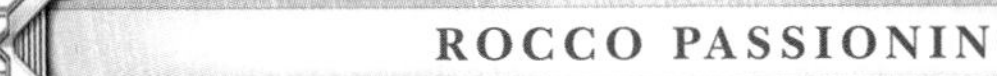

ROCCO PASSIONINO

As the digital visual effects supervisor on the Emmy-winning Zoic team that created the *Firefly* pilot 'Serenity', Rocco Passionino was in charge of guiding the team of artists that translated Carey Meyer and Loni Peristere's designs and concept sketches into the finished CG ships and vehicles featured in the episode.

As the visual effects supervisor on *Angel*, Passionino says it was exciting to follow Whedon to his next creative endeavor. "I had such a strong feeling for Joss's work to begin with, so it was nice to jump onto a pilot he was doing, and for it to be sci-fi which was fantastic because... who doesn't like sci-fi?"

He continues, "*Firefly* gave us the opportunity to do something that had never been done before. It was this fun sci-fi show that we could geek out over back at the office creating wacky space ships we would then deliver back to Joss."

Detailing his responsibilities, Passionino explains, "Because this was such a CG-heavy show, my role as the digital visual effects supervisor was paying attention to the 3-D and the 2-D sides of things, so that Loni could focus on creating. He was doing a lot of the artistic stuff, so my role was after everything was created, was, 'How do we execute it?' As far as the design of the space ships, a lot of that was taking what the art department had done and fleshing it out and giving it a little bit more life. With it being the large show that it was, it was tricky for us to do a lot of that stuff. My job was focusing the vision that both Joss and Loni had for the show into a physical constraint. A lot of what I was doing was making sure the CG could be created and that the composites could be completed the way they were."

From day one, Passionino says the visual effects required for the series were ambitious. "At the time, it was very difficult, but the team was so brilliant about everything. I know a lot of people say that," he laughs, "but I have worked with bad teams before. But the guys on *Firefly* loved the show, and they had a lot of freedom. I think having that freedom to allow their creativity to happen and not have the supervisors jamming things down their throats allowed them to offer ideas and we'd pitch them."

Passionino says another aspect of *Firefly*'s visual effects was that they were always in service of the story, a rarity in sci-fi film and TV, where the initial impulse is often to dazzle. "When you are in the thick of a show, you don't think of the grander scheme of things, or the impact some of these shows will have. But it was great for us to do a sci-fi show on a network channel. We really loved that it was well-written drama. A lot of the visual effects we were doing helped that along, but they weren't the focus of the show. They weren't in your face. It wasn't about the space ships; rather it was about the drama between the actors, which was great. That's what visual effects are supposed to be about. Effects should be about augmenting, not shove-it-in-your-face graphics."

❖ Opposite: Designs for the Dortmunder by Tim Earls.

❖ Above left: Frames from Charles Ratteray's storyboard for the introduction of the Dortmunder.

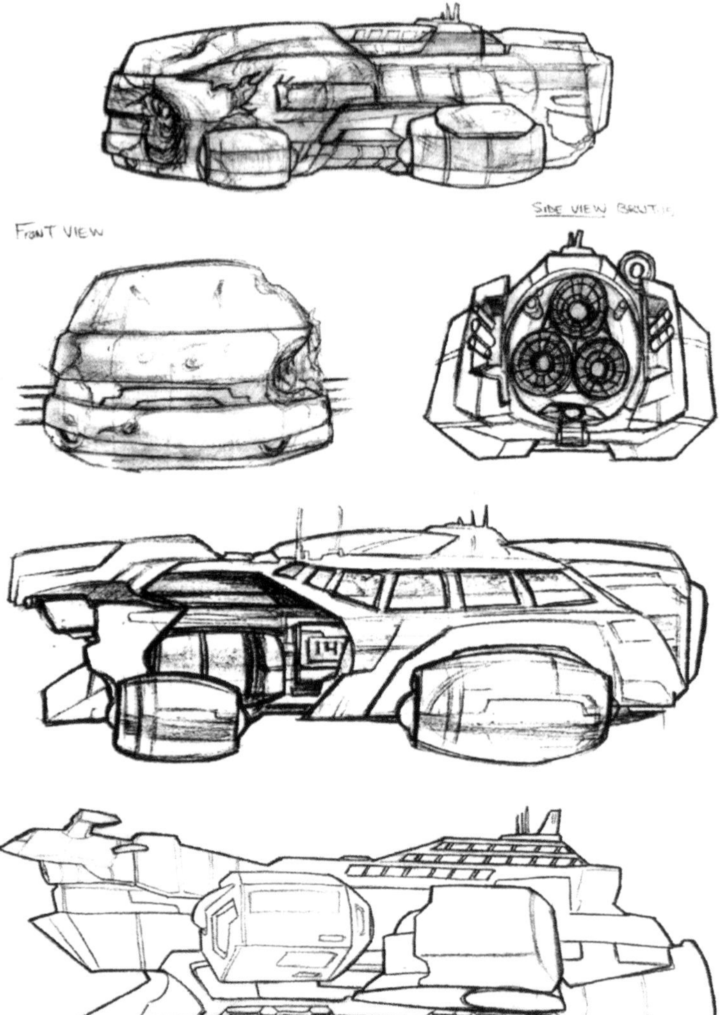

PERSEPHONE'S EAVESDOWN DOCKS

In the episode 'Serenity', Mal's crew lands at a quasi-Skid Row-type docking station filled with a motley assortment of ships. Peristere says all of those vehicles were designed and created for the scene. "Between our department and Carey's department we threw around different sketches for that particular place. We asked what other kinds of ships would you find there? We came up with transportation vessels for people and other kinds of cargo ships. We pulled a bunch of real-world reference and then started deconstructing that material. It became a first set of library rules [vehicles] that inform the series."

MEDSHIP

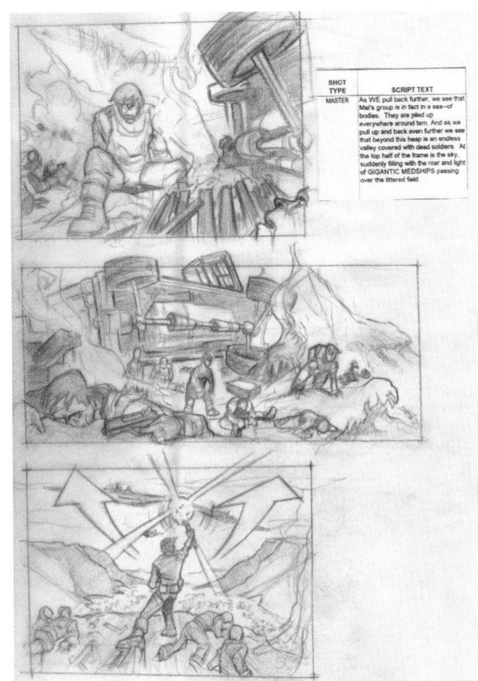

SHOT TYPE
SCRIPT TEXT
MASTER
As WE pull back further, we see that Mal's group is in fact in a sea--of bodies. They are piled up everywhere around tem. And as we pull up and back even further we see that beyond this heap is an endless valley covered with dead soldiers. At the top half of the frame is the sky, suddenly filling with the roar and light of GIGANTIC MEDSHIPS passing over the littered field.

USMED

FRONT HEAD
LEG CLOSURE
LEG DETAIL

FRONT END
BACK LEGS
BOTTOM VIEW
MEDSHIP

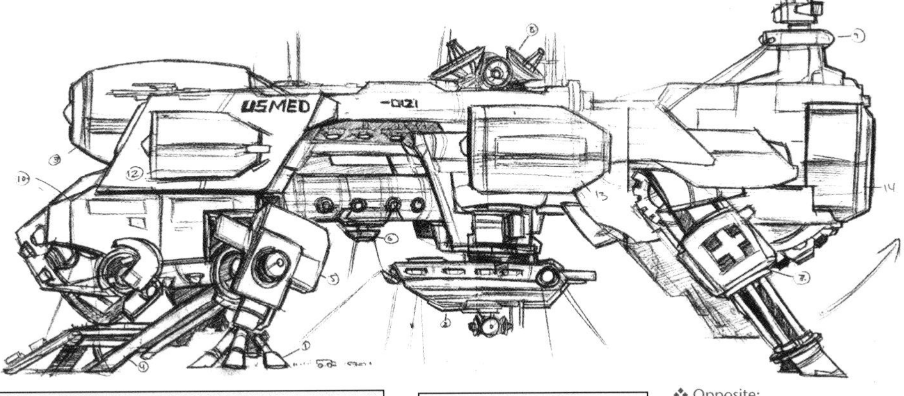

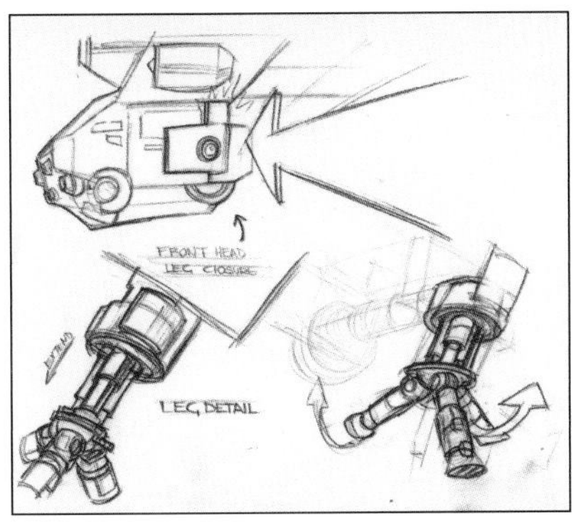

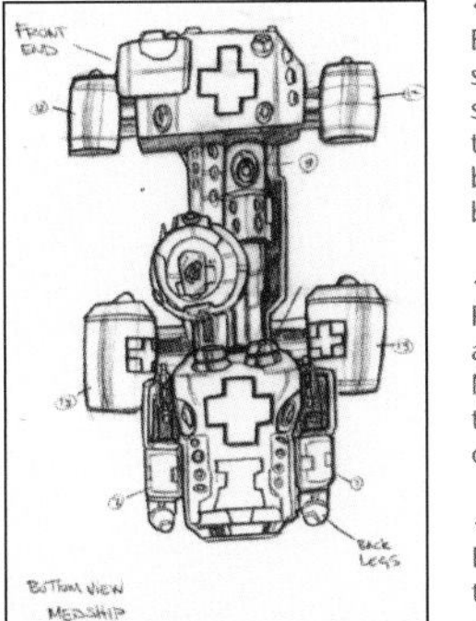

❖ Opposite: Eavesdown docks: A storyboard frame and ship designs (including the Brutus and at the bottom, the Paragon) by Charles Ratteray.

❖ Above and left: Ratteray's storyboard and designs for the Medships glimpsed at the end of the Battle of Serenity.

❖ Below: An early Tim Earls design, adapted to become the Hands of Blue's ship in 'Ariel'.

HANDS OF BLUE SHIP

DOCKING COLLAR
BRIDGE
RCS THRUSTERS
MAIN MOTORS

T. EARLS '02
DORTMUNDER'S VESSELS
FIREFLY
5 FEB '02

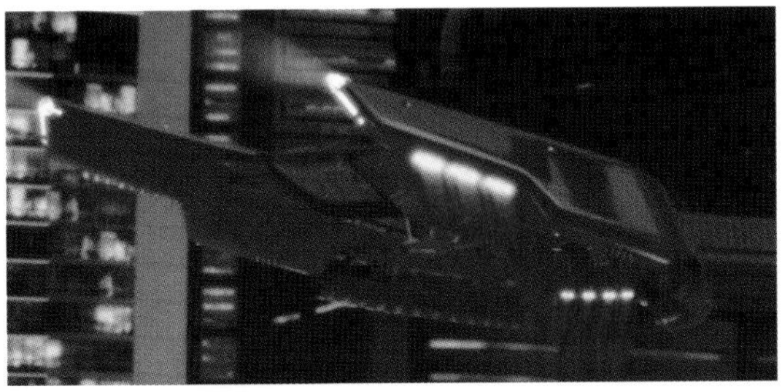

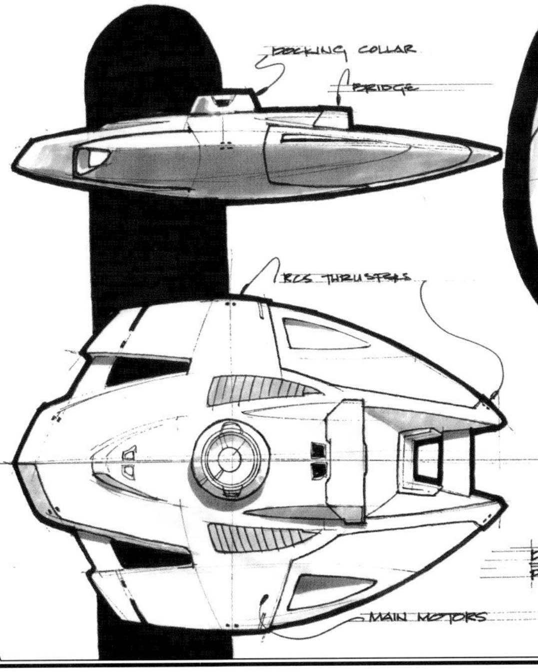

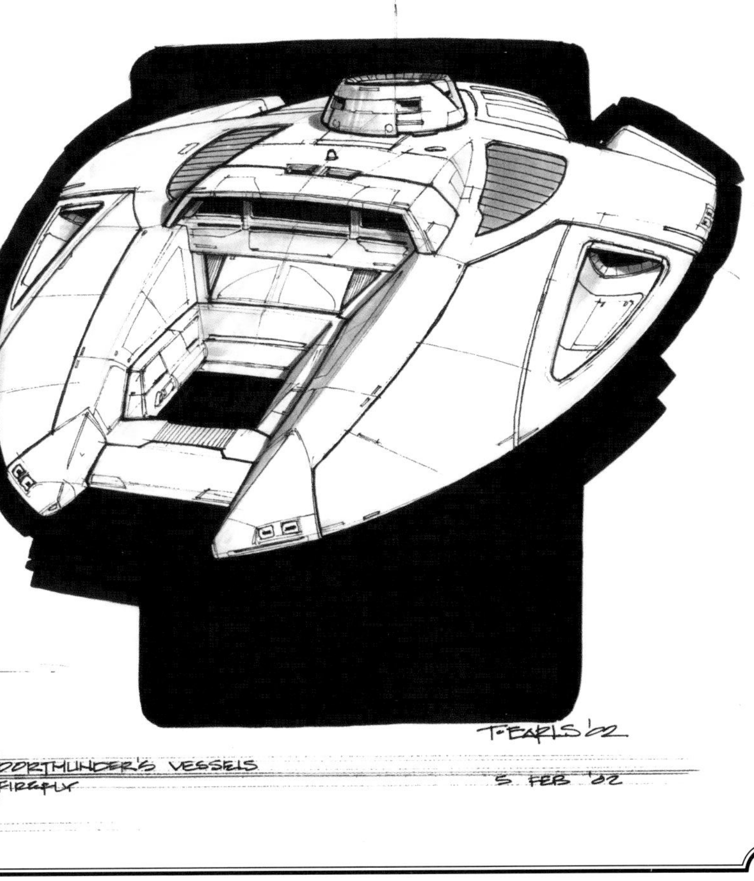

"Loni Peristere is a mad genius, which, apart from his endless attempts to destroy Metropolis, is useful. He and Zoic have provided the best digital effects I've ever seen on TV, which is *very* useful. They've been integral in creating a look, a style – in point of fact, a world. I couldn't imagine having done it without them."

JOSS WHEDON

INTERVIEW WITH AWN.COM, 2002

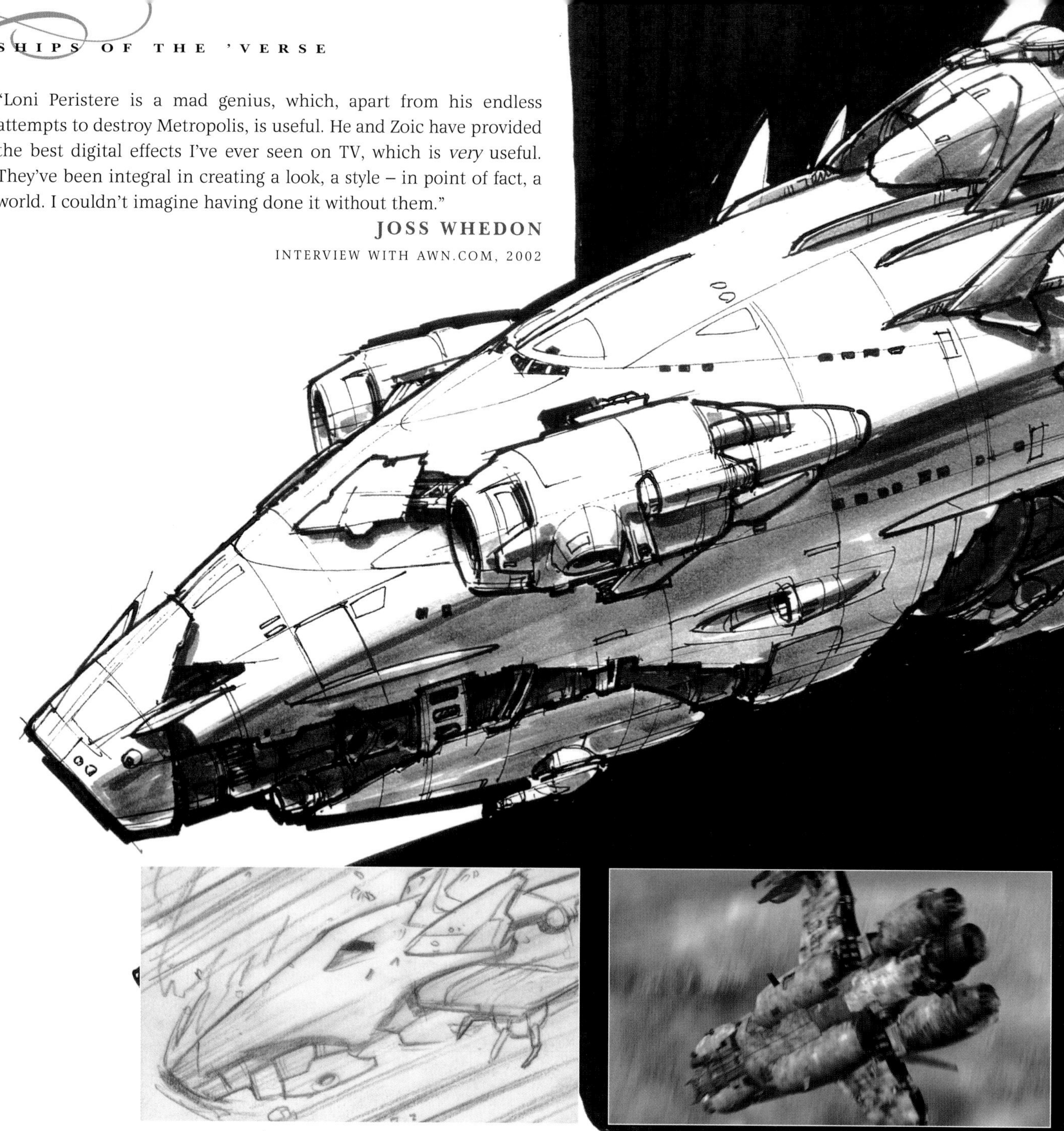

❖ Top: Design for the Reaver ship by Tim Earls.

❖ Above: A storyboard frame by Charles Ratteray from the Reaver chase, and the onscreen result.

REAVER SHIPS

To represent the nightmarish savages that terrorize the outer planets, it was essential for Meyer and Zoic to come up with a visual concept for the Reavers' ships that was just as terrifying as the monsters that lurk within.

"We said that Serenity is this rough-and-tumble ship patched together with pieces of another ship; but it was all from another Firefly class ship," Meyer says about their design rationale. "With the Reaver ship, we decided they would make a ship out of ten ships. The original idea was that the main body was made from a really old super liner cruise ship. They took it and ripped it apart and put engines front, so it was a complete fabrication of ripped-up other ships."

He continues, "Around that time in-house we were building the Serenity interiors on stage and I worked out a short-hand with illustrator Tim Earls, who had finalized some designs for Serenity and the Alliance. He had a good feel for the world we were creating, so when Joss started talking about the Reaver ship, it was literally as quick as saying to Tim, 'Let's go even further than what Serenity was.' We talked about a wide-body 747 and started deconstructing that, along with the idea of a wild boar."

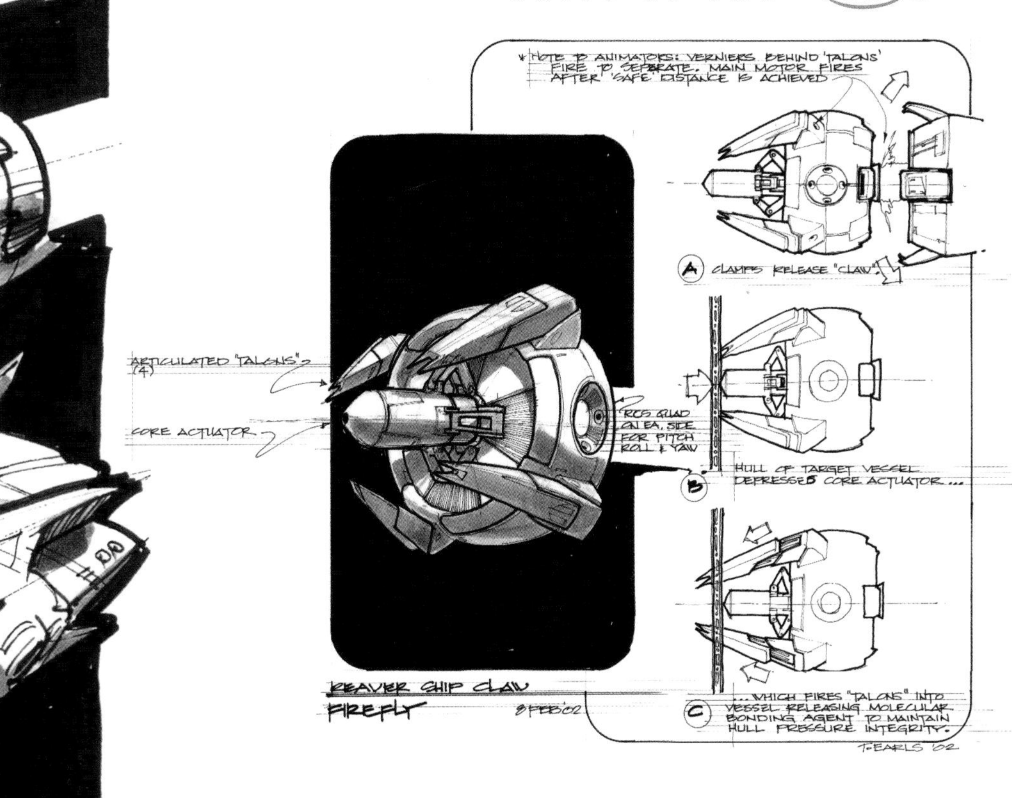
* NOTE TO ANIMATORS: VERNIERS BEHIND 'TALONS' FIRE TO SEPARATE, MAIN MOTOR FIRES AFTER 'SAFE' DISTANCE IS ACHIEVED
A CLAMPS RELEASE "CLAW"
ARTICULATED "TALONS" (4)
CORE ACTUATOR
RCS QUAD ON EA. SIDE FOR PITCH ROLL & YAW
HULL OF TARGET VESSEL
B DEPRESSES CORE ACTUATOR...
C ...WHICH FIRES "TALONS" INTO VESSEL RELEASING MOLECULAR BONDING AGENT TO MAINTAIN HULL PRESSURE INTEGRITY.
REAVER SHIP CLAW
FIREFLY
8FEB'02
T-EARLS '02

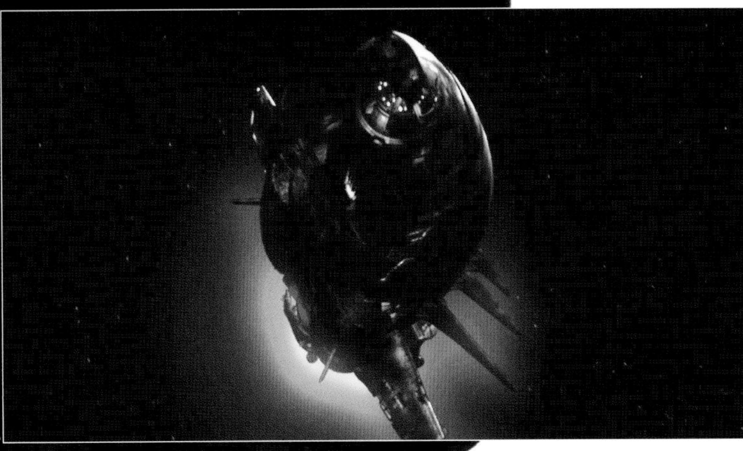
T. EARLS '02

"Then we added the idea they wanted to paint their ships with war paint," Peristere details. "And that they would *purposefully* rip open their containment engine so it would leak. They didn't *care* that they would get radiation poisoning, so the idea was to be as menacing as possible by design. They haphazardly construct the meanest-looking things they can. They create a mask of intimidation so you get scared."

Carey smiles as he remembers, "When I saw the first pre-viz of the Reaver ship chasing Serenity I just about fell out of my chair. It was the coolest thing I had seen in sci-fi."

❖ Top right: The Reavers' grapple claw, as envsioned by Tim Earls.

JUBAL EARLY'S SHIP

The bounty hunter's ship only appeared in 'Objects in Space', but it was an important extension of the charismatic character. Meyer shares, "Ron Cobb [the legendary illustrator who also worked on the likes of *Alien* and *Back to the Future*] worked on that design. Colin DeRune, my art director said to me, 'I have worked with this guy before and he would *love* to design one of these ships.' What I remember about Early's ship was that Joss and Loni kept remarking about Boba Fett's ship Slave One. If you go back and look at the design process for that ship, they took an old sodium vapor light hood and started playing around with it. They flipped it vertically and it looked really cool, so we played around with a similar idea."

THE 'SPACE BAZAAR'

In 'The Message', the Serenity crew visits a space station, described in the script as a Space Bazaar. Inside it's a colorful, bustling marketplace full of people, shops and stalls. The exterior design is similarly striking, and had a very definite inspiration, as Meyer reveals: "It was a whole other idea of how a city in space would work, with bits added on and added on, like the modern day International Space Station works today, as opposed to a thought-out Alliance ship. It wasn't like a Reaver ship, meant to look mean," he clarifies, "but a conglomeration of thousands of people's ideas. We referenced the book *City of Darkness – Life In Kowloon Walled City* [by Ian Lambot and Greg Girard], which is based on a housing development in Hong Kong that had its own police force and its own laws. It was literally this block of humanity that sat in the middle of a city, with its own boundaries. We really went at the bazaar with that book in mind."

THE 'TRASH' FREIGHTER

❖ For 'Trash', Tim Earls designed a full exterior for Monty's freighter, though ultimately only the underside and landing struts were seen.

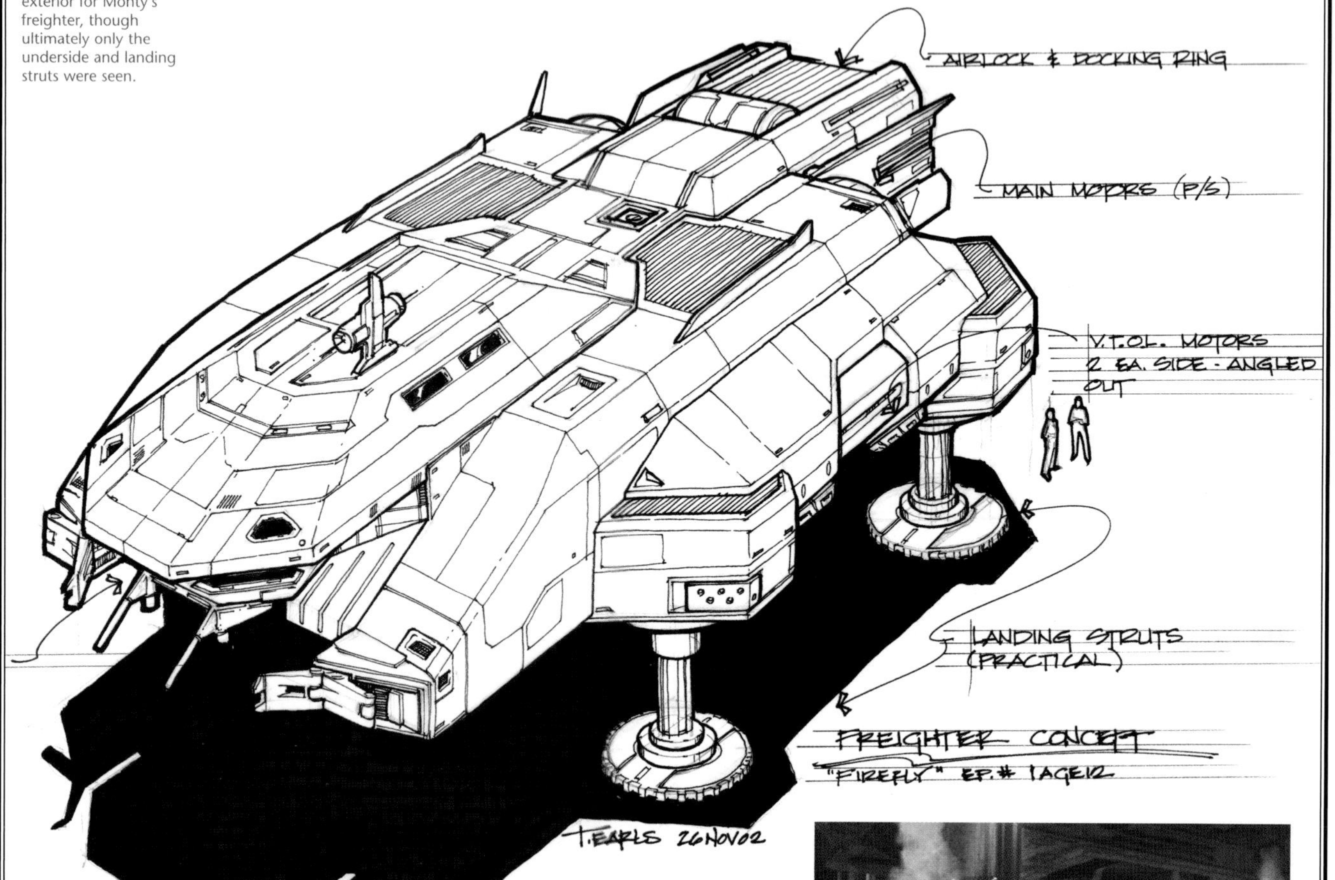

NISKA'S SKYPLEX

For the episodes 'The Train Job' and 'War Stories', the design team needed to create a space station that was a contrast to the Alliance ships, but with a menace all its own. Meyer explains, "It was another design that was both an exterior CG model and interior sets – especially for 'War Stories'. But Loni just took it to the nth degree on the outside."

Peristere continues, "For this space station we imagined that an independent contractor had taken it over, and it had been retrofitted many times. It's almost like a house you rebuild five or six times, and then Serenity has to squeeze and slide in. We created these tubes that were like a claw that would grab Serenity and take it into its folds; inside a deep, dark place."

Meyer says his favorite design aspect was featured inside the station. "The whole station had a central core of a long, long tube that everything glommed onto. Loni knocked it out of the park in Niska's office when they throw the guy over the balcony and you look down and it's basically that core. Amazing."

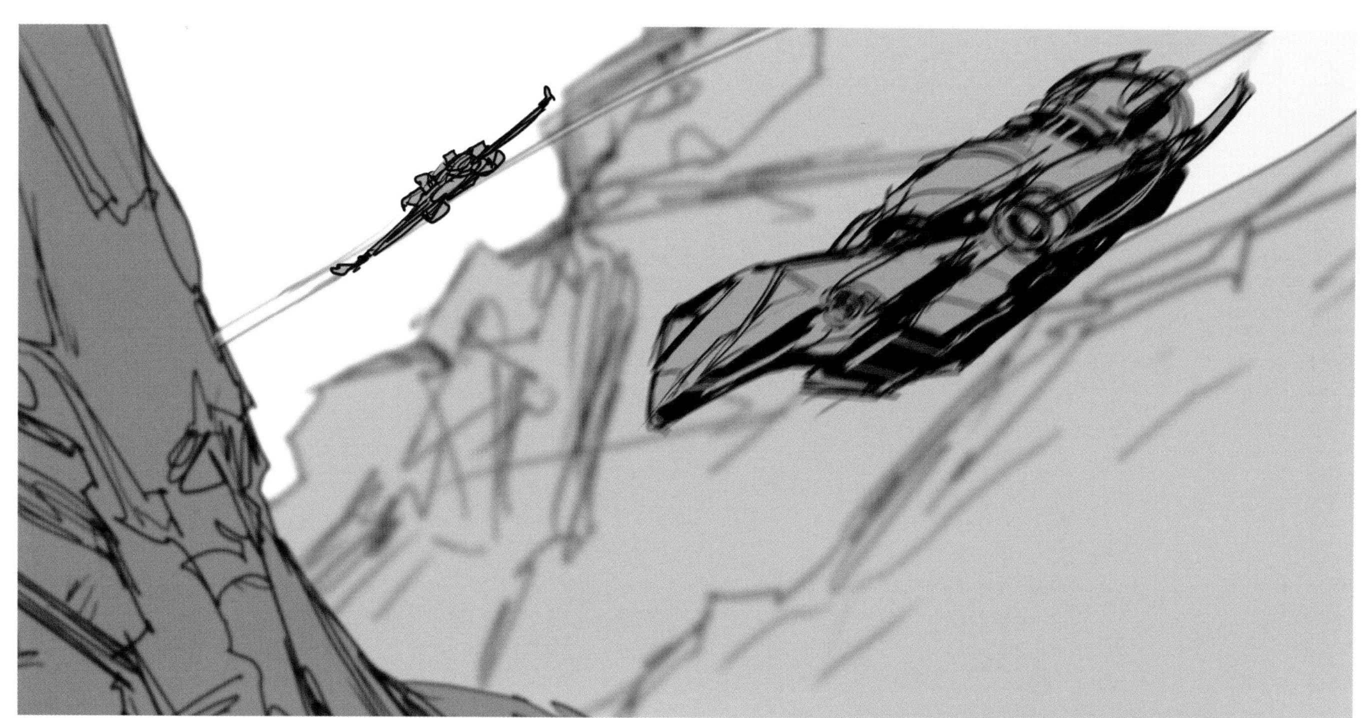

ALLIANCE SHORT RANGE ENFORCEMENT VESSEL (ASREV)

These small gun ships were housed within the larger Alliance vessels, and were originally glimpsed in 'Trash' before one had a starring role in the memorable chase sequence in 'The Message'. Meyer explains that these ships represented the point where he handed off the intricate design work to the Zoic team.

"We were so deep into production of the show that Loni completely took over in terms of getting the design process finished on these kinds of vehicles," Meyer explains.

"So we brought in some superstar freelance designers [like Ron Cobb] to help us out," Peristere continues. "With this ship, the idea was to take technology of today and advance it several hundred years and imagine what would be functional both in space and in atmosphere. I wanted to think about what would work in both spaces. Again we employed a joint strike fighter VTOL system where a panel opened up in the wing so it could lift off vertically instead of needing a runway. At the same time we wanted a sleek, bad-ass look that was intimidating and looked like a creature. We wanted it to be familiar, yet fresh and functional."

❖ Opposite and below: Charles Ratteray's storyboards for the chase sequence in 'The Message'.

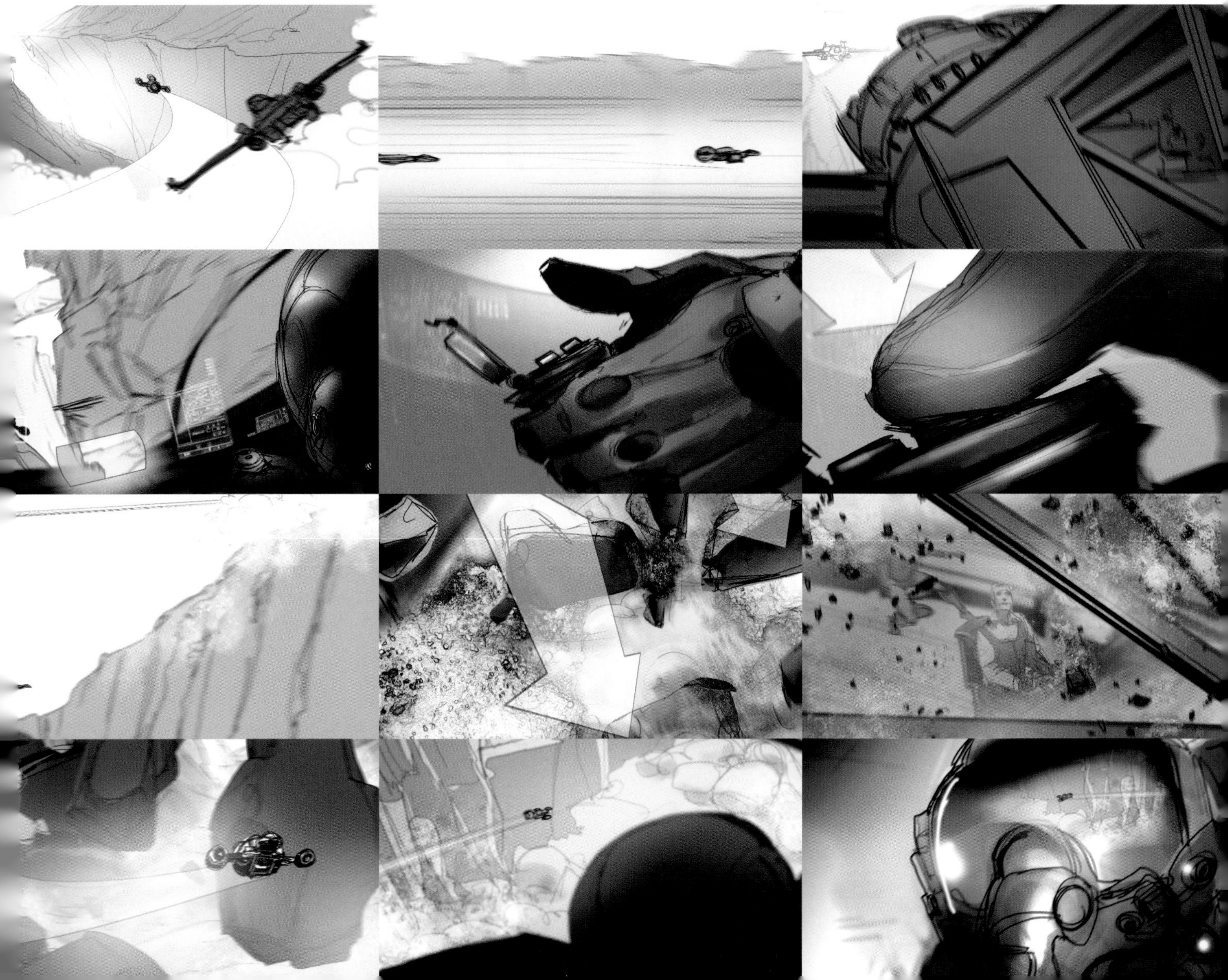

RON GLASS

Shepherd Derrial Book

RON ON THE CAST:

From the very beginning it was like... people were perfectly cast. Everybody was slightly different but were versatile and had a good work ethic. It was a very harmonious atmosphere to work in.

INTERVIEW WITH FRACTALMATTER.COM, 2006

ON EMBRACING FANDOM:

I'm surprised that the popularity lingers. It was very fulfilling but I've never been associated with a show that did conventions. Yeah, they're quite wonderful. The people have a reputation for being... let's just say the reputation is not totally sane, but there's the other side that I think is very warm and really gentle. So I feel privileged to be able to partake in it. In a certain kind of way, the *Firefly* fans are much more informed and aware about the *Firefly* universe than I am. In a way they are more interested. Most of the sci-fi genre can be a large part of their lives. For me, I just slipped into it, I was just fascinated by the characterisation, but again, I'm grateful for it and it's opened my perspective in ways that I couldn't have anticipated.

INTERVIEW WITH FRACTALMATTER.COM, 2006

RON GLASS

NATHAN FILLION ON RON:

"I could listen to Ron Glass read the phone book. When you ask Ron Glass a question he does this [impersonates Ron deep in thought] and then he answers you. He's always connected, he's always connecting and I just admire him. He's a smart guy and he picks his moments and he's always shiny."

SPEAKING ON STAGE AT THE 'SERENITY' CONVENTION, 2005

GINA TORRES ON RON:

I adore Ron. I was watching Ron as most people of our generation were on *Barney Miller* – my earliest memories of television. When he walked on stage for the first time when we did the series, I was like, "I love you!"

INTERVIEW WITH BLACKFILM.COM, 2005

THE CAST DISCUSS MEETING RON FOR THE FIRST TIME, AND DISCOVERING HIS UNIQUE SENSE OF HUMOR:

Jewel: [Ron] just appeared to be very zen and calm and kind and genuine. It's true he is. And then we got to know him and this twisted, sick sense of humor came out. It came out of nowhere.

Nathan: And you'll never see it coming...

Jewel: You won't see it coming. He'll say the sickest, funniest, most insulting thing and we'll just be on the floor laughing.

Morena: I just have to tell my Ron story. We're standing doing a shoot for 'Heart of Gold', in what's supposed to be the tinfoil whore house and I'm standing there in my normal Inara outfit which was always more extravagant than everybody else's, who are all in canvas pants or overalls or whatever. And I see Ron looking at me from across the room kind of like [shakes head] and I walk up to him and I'm like, "Hi Ron!" and he says [about Inara's costume], "What is this? A f***ing carnival act?"

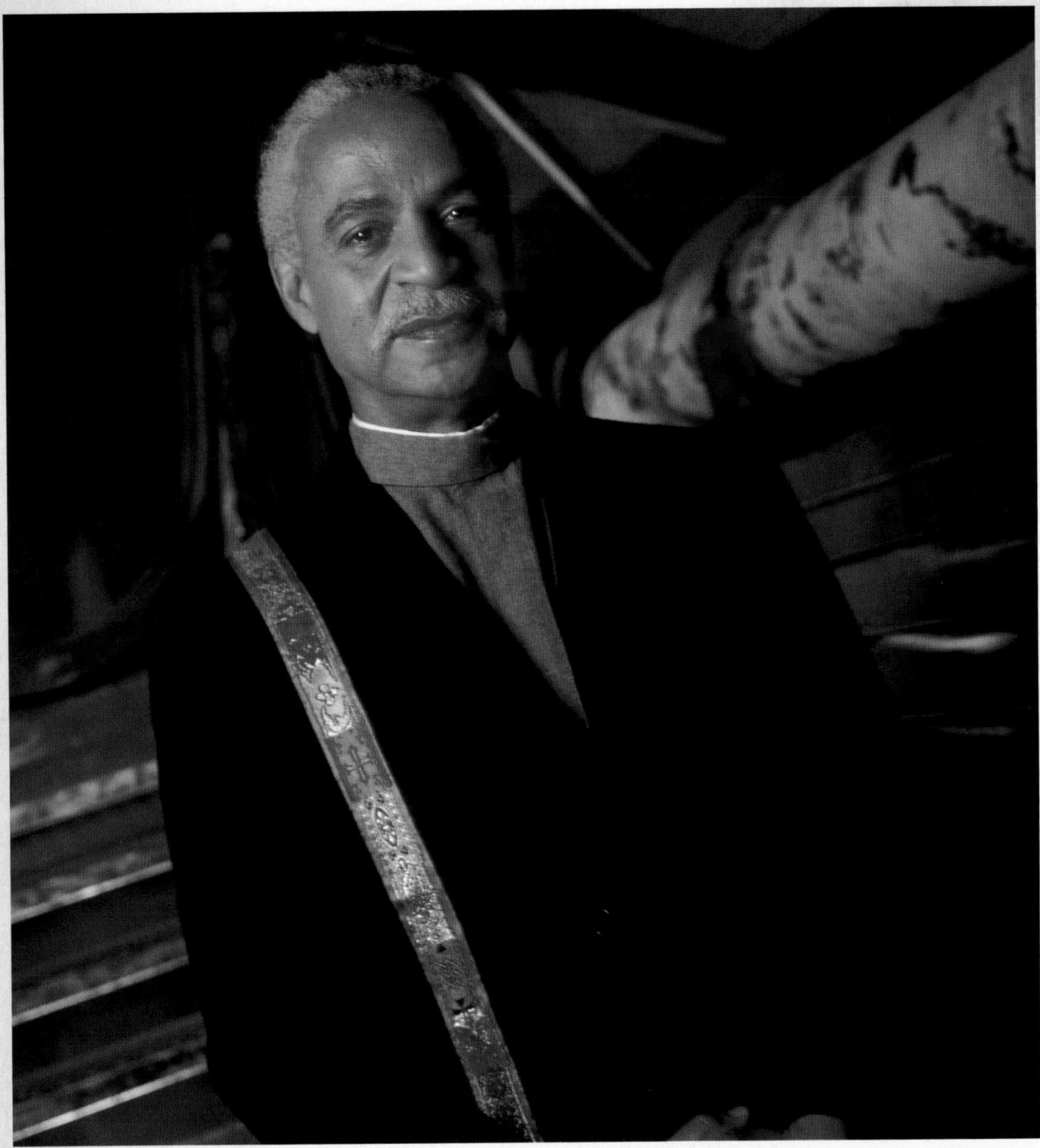

Jewel: And yesterday when we were all sort of reunited here in the UK [for the convention], Ron came up to Morena and looked her up and down and gave her a hug and said, "Hi honey, so where are the elephants?"

SPEAKING ON STAGE AT THE 'SERENITY' CONVENTION, 2005

RON'S ANSWER WHEN ASKED AT A CONVENTION WHAT HE KNOWS OF BOOK'S BACKSTORY:

This whole experience of dealing with fans in a convention environment was totally new for me. The very first convention that I went to was in England, and somebody asked me that question, and I said, "Well actually I think that Book, before he became a Shepherd, was a choreographer." So I'm going to stick with that! [Laughs].

SPEAKING ON STAGE AT THE DALLAS COMIC CON, 2006

A STORY HE WAS TOLD BY A FAN:

This guy was telling me he'd been to a place where you could get used DVDs, and he was standing there in line waiting to check out, and some woman is going through a box, and she picks up a used DVD. It turns out that it was a copy of *Serenity*, and she yelled really loud in the store, "Whoever brought this here is going to *hell*!"

SPEAKING ON STAGE AT THE DALLAS COMIC CON, 2006

THE BROWNCOATS

An overview of Firefly fandom

Below: *Firefly* in space! In June 2007, Astronaut and Browncoat Steven Swanson, pictured here with Sunita Williams, took a set of DVDs to the International Space Station on NASA Shuttle mission STS-117.

WRITER AND EXECUTIVE PRODUCER TIM MINEAR

What is there to say about the fandom? *Firefly* has got its own vibe. It's a little bit different than the other stuff. I mean, I have been involved in stuff that has been very fan-friendly. Everything from *Lois & Clark*, *The X-Files* to *Angel*, but for some reason, the *Firefly* fans are their own special thing. And it could be because it was killed so early – there's a sort of tragedy to the whole thing [laughs]. If only the network had the tiniest bit of farsightedness that the fans of *Firefly* have shown over the last five years, then we'd probably be in our sixth or seventh season by now. But we love the fans and we love the show, too. We are fans as well.

INTERVIEW WITH ABBIE BERNSTEIN, 2009.

Firefly fans, universally known as the Browncoats, have a special place in sci-fi fandom. This brief overview can only hope to scratch the surface of the story of how they have kept the show alive in the years since cancellation, but one thing's for sure: you can't stop the signal!

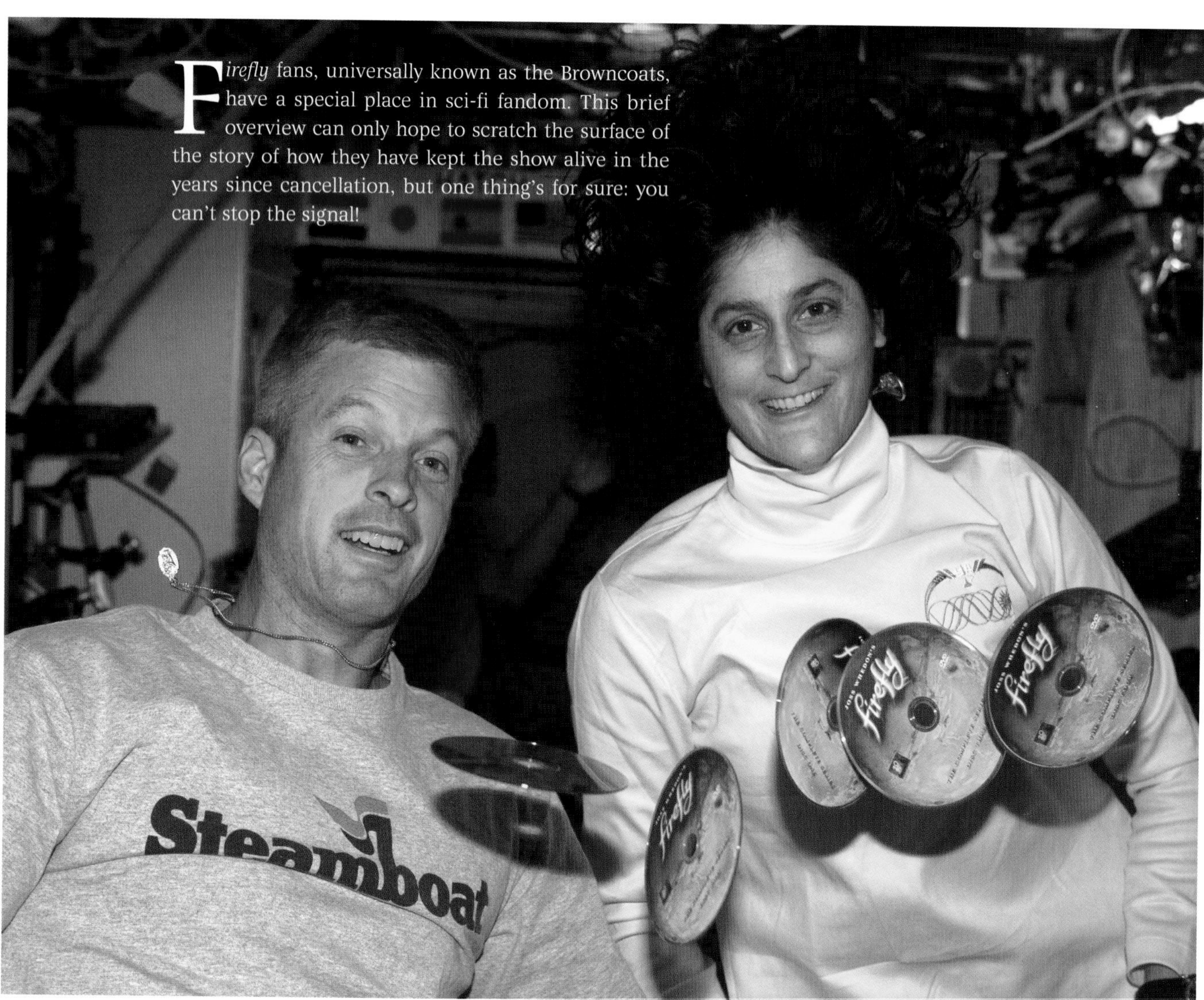

CONVENTIONS

While the Internet is certainly integral to *Firefly* fandom, if one wants to encounter a cross-section of ardent Browncoats in the same place at the same time, there's nothing like a convention. Creation Entertainment's Salute to *Firefly* and *Serenity* at the LAX Marriott in November 2009 had an impressive guest list, including Morena Baccarin, Adam Baldwin, Jewel Staite, Mark Sheppard and Alan Tudyk (who ran an impromptu trivia quiz and gave out *Firefly*-related prizes for the right answers), and writers Jane Espenson and Tim Minear. The convention was abuzz with fans who had come from not only all over the country, but all over the world, both to see the guests and to visit with one another.

Wendy Scott has come from England, where she runs a *Firefly/Serenity* podcast called Sending the Wave. Describing the appeal of *Firefly* fandom, Scott says, "For a start, it's so much fan-led. The great thing is certainly everybody here, seriously, within thirty seconds, you know them. They're so friendly, they're so open. It's kind of like we've bonded in the trenches of Serenity Valley," she laughs. "We all share this very, very precious thing, and it's great when we get feedback from the podcast and we know that there are so many people listening to it across the world. We feel that we're doing our part to keep the fandom going. I've loved Westerns since I was a child and when I first saw the pilot, I genuinely wasn't sure if I was going to like it, but when we got to Eavesdown Docks, it was, 'Oh, my God, I know this place,' because I was a huge *Star Wars* fan. To me, that was Mos Eisley. I see *Firefly* as *Star Wars*' first cousin. And I thought, 'Oh, I'm home.' And then it just kept going. I think we had something very precious in the episodes that we had. It was very rich, and you can keep going back."

Nicole Hoye is an Australian currently living in Toronto. She says her UK friends also attending the convention persuaded her to come to Los Angeles for the event. "I had been to a couple of the Starfury [*Firefly* conventions] in the UK, so that's how I met all of those friends. So I came along to this one to see them, and the guests, and to see what a US convention is like. It's been great. Really good panels and the dealer room is *amazing*." Hoye says she is attracted to *Firefly* because of "the characters. It's a really character-driven story. Sometimes I find with a lot of sci-fi that it tends to roll around the setting and idea of, 'Oh, it's sci-fi' so much that *Firefly* really stands on its own."

A woman who goes by the *Nom de Web* Raven

❖ Above: Nathan Fillion meets the fans at San Deigo Comic-Con 2009.

❖ Left: Tim Minear (center) with the California Browncoats (CABC) team at Comic-Con 2007.

❖ Top: "Check this out, I rock at these," Nathan Fillion told fan Sean Koo as he took this photo for him.

❖ Right: The CABC in action at Wondercon 2009.

❖ Below: Would you buy a T-shirt from this man? Adam Baldwin helps out on the CABC stand at Wondercon 2009.

Underwood has come to the convention from Chicago, Illinois. She's been involved in all the Joss Whedon-related fandoms and, in her opinion, "The difference between *Firefly* and a lot of the other ones is, it's sci-fi. It hit a chord with sci-fi people. And there are a lot more costumes involved," she notes with a laugh. "I think because it was canceled so quickly, this is something special. Like *Star Trek* was in the sixties, *Firefly* is in the 2000s, they're similar in that respect, fighting to keep it alive. These convention events do that, as well as everything the fans are doing, and it brings a lot of people together."

Tony Arlen has traveled from Northern California. This is his first convention. "This is the first time I've ever done anything like this. And it's kind of scary – I came by myself, I couldn't talk my wife into coming. I'm just kind of star-struck and very shy but trying to do my best to really enjoy everything. *Firefly* – I can't stop watching it. I love it. It's very real and very honest – even though it's set in space and it's 500 years from now. I feel a lot of chemistry, a family atmosphere, among the characters, among the actors. And I read something in [one of the previous *Firefly* volumes] that Christina Hendricks said, that she felt so warm and welcomed when she came and did her guest shots on the show, which was not the case for a lot of her guest-starring work. So that's the feeling I get – it's family."

CHARITY

Browncoats are very active in fundraising for good causes. Many of these are favorites of Whedon and the cast. Whedon is a proponent of Equality Now, an organization that promotes women's rights worldwide, which has been the beneficiary of Browncoat-raised funds. Ron Glass has brought attention to the Al Wooten Jr Heritage Center in South Central Los Angeles, which helps underprivileged children; Adam Baldwin has spoken up for the Marine Corps and Law Enforcement Foundation, which raises money to help the children of fallen US military and law enforcement personnel; Jewel Staite is a proponent of the Dyslexia Foundation. All of these and more have received monies raised at Browncoat-sponsored events.

James Riley, president of the California Browncoats, explains this is both fun and a serious business. "As a non-profit corporation, we have existed since June 2007. Our main purpose is to raise funds for the charities selected by the cast and crew of *Firefly* and *Serenity*, and we do that by running fan tables at conventions like Creation's and Wonder-Con and Comic-Con. I'd have to go look at the spreadsheet again, but I'm pretty sure since

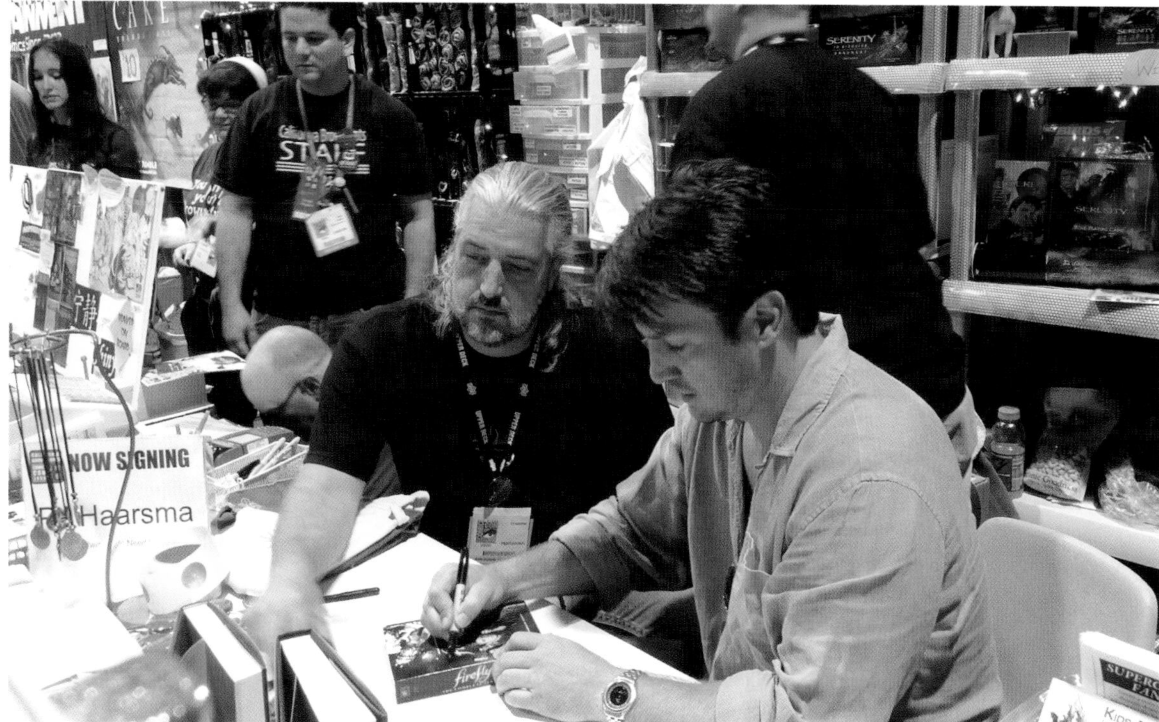

2007, the California Browncoats alone have raised close to $100,000 for charity, and Browncoats as a whole I think have raised somewhere close to half a million dollars for charity."

Riley continues, "I think the best thing about *Firefly* and *Serenity* is not the fact that the fandom for the show has lasted so long, but that the community that was built around the show has lasted too. I think that's why it's lasted so long, because the Browncoats themselves have kept it alive. Don't get me wrong, the performers and writers are definitely all a very large part of it, but not since some other key fandoms like *Star Wars* and *Star Trek* has there been a fandom built around the fandom itself and the community that it has developed. The need to do good seems to have developed inside the community itself. The Backup Bash [a convention set up literally at the last minute, when a major *Firefly* convention fell apart the day it was supposed to begin] was definitely something that brought a lot of the fans closer together, it kind of made us huddle around ourselves instead of relying on others, and I think it showed that we could do things if we had to."

Beth Nelson, a New Yorker who has relocated to Austin, Texas, is one of the Austin Browncoats. She's involved with both the charitable "Can't Stop the Serenity" screenings and licensed *Firefly/Serenity* collectibles. "I've been a fan since the very beginning. I'm a huge space Western fan, so I had to get involved. Charity-wise, I started getting really active in 2007. There is one global organizer who usually has a team that helps them run the events, and then each city has their own organizer. And so we try to keep it very central. Everybody has similar rules, but we get to put a lot of individual thought into each event, so that they're unique."

Kids Need to Read is a charity started in 2007 by author P.J. Haarsma and Nathan Filllion, with assistance from Alan Tudyk and many Browncoats. Denise Gary, the organization's executive director, explains how Kids began and what it does. "P.J. Haarsma has a children's sci-fi book. He's gone around to schools presenting his book and found out that a lot of them didn't have any funding for new books. It was a large problem. Haarsma is very good friends with Nathan Fillion and actually Alan Tudyk as well. He went to Nathan and asked if he would be interested in helping solve this problem. Nathan said, 'You bet, I want to help.' P.J. came to me, because I had a group of Browncoats that had worked with him before on another project, and asked if we would like to also help and make his vision come about. We are based out of Phoenix, Arizona, but we are a national program. Our core program is to buy new books for under-funded schools and libraries and clinics and shelters, any place that has a good literacy program for children, especially disadvantaged children. It is also about giving the right kind of books. Most of our kids are very underprivileged, very poverty-stricken, they're not surrounded with a culture of reading. So we give books that have valuable substance and a lot of uplifting messages. That's a very big part of our mission as well. The core people running the charity are Browncoats, and most of the volunteers that we have coming in are Browncoats, who hear about Kids Need to Read and want to help."

Why is Gary a Browncoat? "Oh, because *Firefly* to me is simply unforgettable. I cannot get it out of my system. It's just a part of me."

Above: Nathan and Kids Need to Read founder P. J. Haarsma sign for fans at the 2008 Comic-Con.

MERCHANDISE

Whether it's a fan-made costume or prop replica, or a professional licensed product, *Firefly* has inspired an outpouring of creativity, including artwork, models, podcasts, audio plays, a role-playing game, 'Filk' music, even Serenity-shaped cakes. On the pro side, a highlight came in 2005 when Dark Horse Comics teamed with Joss Whedon to bring forth *Those Left Behind*, a three-issue chronicle of the adventures of our Big Damn Heroes between the events of *Firefly* and *Serenity*. Written by Whedon and Brett Matthews, with art from Will Conrad, it was a great success, leading to follow-up *Better Days* in 2008, with *Float Out* and *A Shepherd's Tale* announced for 2010.

Quantum Mechanix, or QMx for short, is a licensed collectibles/props replica company that came into being in 2005 out of love for *Firefly*. CEO Andy Gore relates, "*Firefly* was the sole reason why I got into it. I had actually not been in the collectibles business previously, but I have a fairly extensive background in web development. The founders of the company wanted me to build the interactive strategy for the company and I basically said, 'Well, you can pay me,' and what I normally get paid was way more than they could afford, 'or you can pick up the *Serenity* license.' And they said, 'Okay, we'll pick up the *Serenity* license.' So I basically traded a website for the opportunity to do the things that I'm doing now. We only just picked up the *Firefly* license, but we've been interested in it for a long time. We have a lot of stuff in development. Our categories include prop replicas, ship replicas, T-shirts, posters, maquettes [small statue likenesses of the characters], key chains and bumper stickers and so forth."

Fans are very involved in QMx product development, Gore adds. "As a matter of fact, we developed a secure confidential collaboration space online where we invite particularly dedicated fans to come in and look at early versions of the products we're developing and let us know what they think and give us advice, catch mistakes. A number of the products we do are very, very detailed and they take years to create, and so there are lots of opportunities for fans to give input and also, frankly, to find errors when they happen. These cutaways," Gore indicates a series of detailed plans of Serenity and other 'verse craft, "are only four pages, but there are thousands of pieces of information in them, and while we have a wonderful research team and we're lucky to be working with the production designers from both the movie and the series [Geoffrey Mandel and Timothy Earls], even they will tell you that the fans find things that they've missed. So we're very engaged with the fan community. In terms of what they're like, fans aren't shy about letting you know what they're interested in. Fans oftentimes have some of the best ideas. But in a sense, we're fans as well, and so I almost view it as a collaboration with the community."

In at least one case, QMx has afforded the opportunity for a fan artist to turn pro. Gore explains, "Adam Levermore started as a fan designer, but – I will quote a Hollywood designer who works with us on a regular basis – 'There are fan designers who are incredibly skilled and the only real difference between them and a quote-unquote professional is knowledge of the franchise.' Oftentimes, the fan designer is every bit as good as the

❖ Above: A Captain and his ship. Nathan Fillion meets QMx's 'Big Damn Replica' of Serenity, seen in detail opposite.

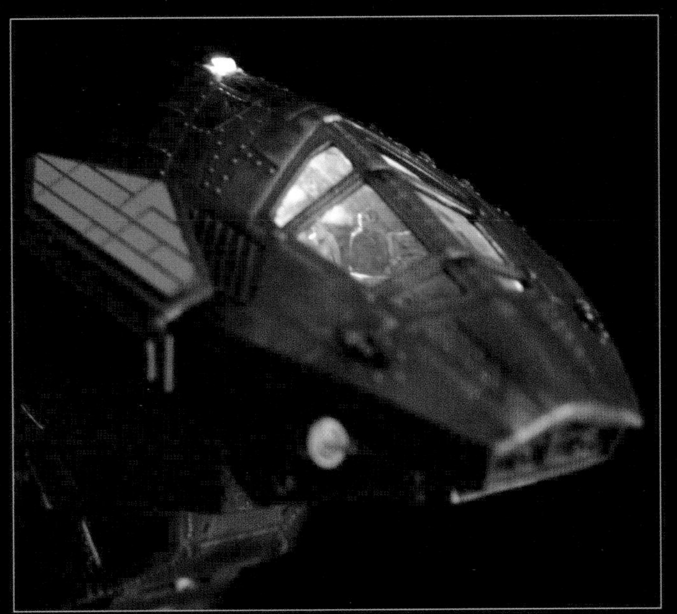

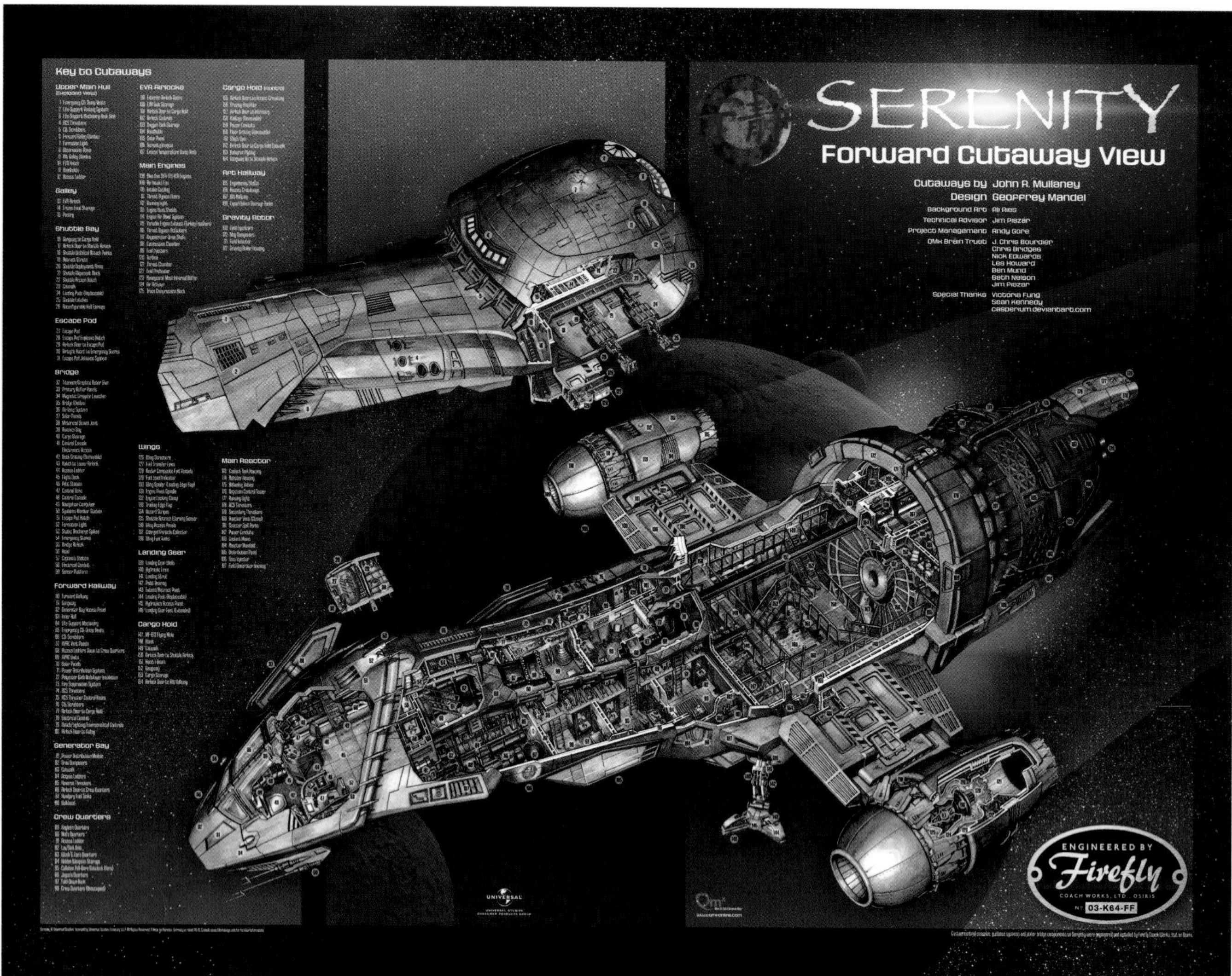

❖ Above: One of QMx's ultra-detailed Serenity cutaways.

professional, but the fan knows more about the material. So we love fan designers. Not all of them are working at that level of skill, but the ones who are ultimately end up being the best designers to work with."

Levermore connected with Gore at the Backup Bash, where QMx needed dealer space at the last minute and Levermore had a table for his fan art company, Black Market Beagles. Levermore recalls, "Andy came and we talked and really got along well. He asked if I was interested in doing some work for them and it grew from there." He believes his artwork, largely of 'verse ships, props and locations, has improved since joining the company. "It ramped up very quickly. I've always doodled and sketched, but I'd never really worked professionally, certainly never selling any of my art before Black Market Beagles, and when I got together with QMx, it took a big jump from there as well, getting to work on officially licensed stuff for *Firefly* and *Serenity*, and also *Battlestar Galactica* and *Star Trek* and *Stargate: SG-1*, so it's been really exciting and fast-paced and I've really enjoyed working with them."

Like James Riley, Levermore says he feels the fan-run, totally not-for-profit Backup Bash was a major event for the Browncoats. "There's no question. It's something that I think changed a lot of people's lives and set a lot of things in motion in terms of what people were doing with the fandom and how they felt about it. For me personally, I made a lot of contacts through it, a lot of new friends, a lot of memories, but I think everybody who was involved in it, whether they were involved in arranging it or just participating in it, had an experience of a lifetime."

As for what drew QMx's CEO to *Firefly*, Gore says, "Everything, honestly. *Firefly* will be remembered decades from now as being one of the most innovative pieces of entertainment that was ever done – for its characterization, production design, gritty realism, even the way that the show was shot. I mean, *Battlestar Galactica* is one of the most successful sci-fi series ever, and even they will tell you how much they owe to *Firefly* – Steadicam, ships that don't make noise in space, gritty, realistic, lived-in ship design, sci-fi plots that are character-driven as opposed to technology-driven or scenario-driven, all these things. *Firefly* is literally the Rosetta Stone of what I would consider the modern wave of sci-fi on TV."

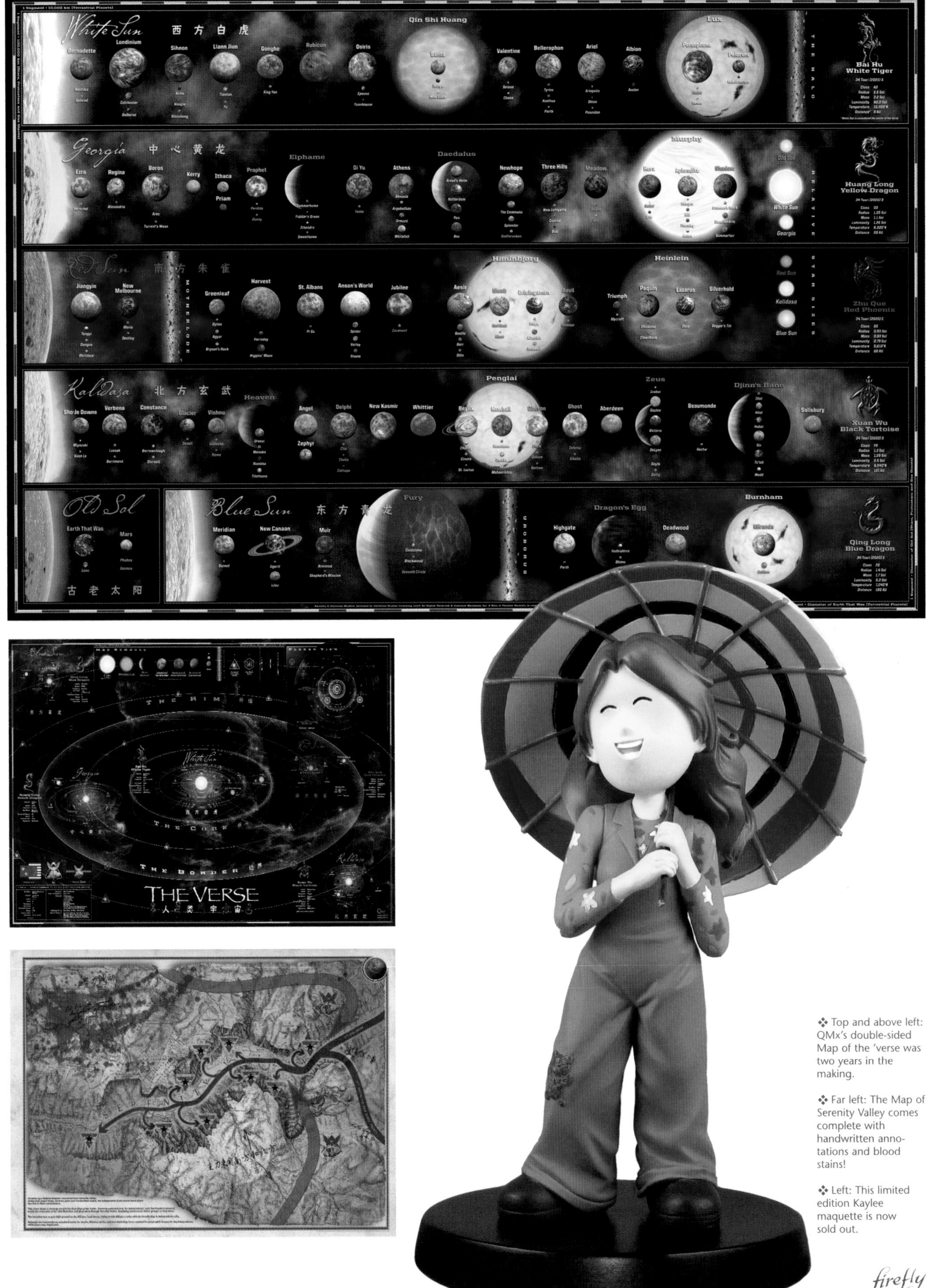

❖ Top and above left: QMx's double-sided Map of the 'verse was two years in the making.

❖ Far left: The Map of Serenity Valley comes complete with handwritten annotations and blood stains!

❖ Left: This limited edition Kaylee maquette is now sold out.

FAN FILMS

In written form, fan fiction – taking the universe and characters created by professionals and coming up with new stories that are distributed not for profit, but simply for the love of doing it – has been around almost as long as fiction. However, filmed fan fiction is relatively new. Fan-made feature-length documentaries aren't quite so rare, but they are still fairly uncommon. However, Browncoat enthusiasm has brought forth a number of cinematic endeavors.

On the documentary side, the best-known Browncoat-made film is *Done The Impossible: The Fans' Tale of Firefly & Serenity*, a chronicle of fan efforts to help *Firefly* continue, culminating with the release of *Serenity*. *Done The Impossible* was produced and directed by the team of Brian Wiser, Jeremy Neish, Jared Nelson, Jason Heppler and Tony Hadlock. Wiser explains their impetus. "We couldn't let the *Firefly* fan community and their major efforts be forgotten. What the fans accomplished and the way they did it was unparalleled and unexpected. We wanted to share the unique journey from *Firefly* to *Serenity* and contribute something to the 'verse that people could enjoy and connect with. Additionally, we wanted to create something for existing Browncoats, as well as people who were new to the 'verse, to keep the Browncoat momentum moving forward."

Done The Impossible began production in 2005. "During that time," Wiser says, "I arranged interviews with fans, cast, crew and executives. We were filming, editing and developing unique special features. We felt it was very important to have someone from the series help convey the story and Adam Baldwin was a perfect fit. When I asked Adam at Dragon Con if he would be willing to host the documentary, he was genuinely interested in a way that demonstrated he not only believed in our film, but in the importance of the message of *Firefly* and the fans. Jewel Staite took her vacation time to record the timeline and trivia voiceover as Kaylee. The fans and cast were incredibly cooperative. People were very eager to share their feelings about why *Firefly* has such a following and how it affected their lives. *Firefly* composer Greg Edmonson invited us into his home and Tim Minear took time away from a very important engagement. I was surprised at how many people had stories and experiences we can all relate to, and how willing and excited people were to be involved. I also contacted Joss and several executives – they were all very supportive of our project."

First screened at Comic-Con in 2006, now available on DVD and with a Blu-ray released in 2010, *Done The Impossible* has played at a number of film festivals around the world and raised money for charity. "Donating to charity is an important part of who the Browncoats are. That's why we initially donated $5,000 to Equality Now. Each year we donate and support charitable events like Can't Stop the Serenity." Wiser says the film has in some instances helped fans find one another. "Fans have found connections to the Browncoat community that they may not have known about if they had only watched *Firefly*." However, most gratifying for Wiser is that "I have enjoyed deep

friendships with fans and cast that have continued to this day. I find many of the relationships I hold most dear have originated through *Firefly*."

Wiser was also one of the organizers of the 2007 Browncoat Cruise, a weeklong floating convention with Ron Glass as a headlining guest, and is one of the producers on *Browncoats: Redemption*, a feature-length narrative film about what happens in the 'verse once it's discovered that the Alliance created the dreaded Reavers through a backfired effort at mind control.

"We took the premise that was already there from the content that's been established so far," reveals *Browncoats: Redemption* writer/director/producer/co-creator Michael C. Dougherty. "It's a new ship and a new crew, on a total opposite end of the 'verse [than Mal Reynolds and the Serenity crew], having to deal with the Alliance and trying to make sense of everything that's going on. For the Core planets, the Alliance is pretending that the information about the Reavers is anti-propaganda, but the Rim planets are all up in arms because they know it's true. You have a crew who normally do the right things, completely unlike Mal, but are now forced to start taking the jobs that Mal would normally take to be able to survive. The story flows from there."

Steven Fisher, the other *Browncoats: Redemption* co-creator/producer, explains the project's origins. "In July 2008, I was talking to a friend who had done a lot of *Star Trek* fan films and we were talking about *Firefly* fan films. At the time, I didn't know there were any, so I thought we should try something like this. I'd known Mike for about six months at the time, and I said, 'I want to do a *Firefly* film.' Mike is a great writer, and we started to work on this together. We obviously didn't want to impinge on anything that Joss was going to create with his crew, so what we did was to create a new crew and tell a different perspective."

Whedon gave his blessing, Dougherty relates. We [Dougherty and Fisher] agreed that we couldn't go forward without letting Joss know. I finally got Joss's assistant on the phone and did our pitch in about fifteen seconds flat without breathing, and when she stopped laughing, she said, 'Slow down, say it again.' I told her what we were trying to do. She said, 'Send a detailed email. I'll get you a response one way or the other.' After a month and a half of pins and needles waiting, we finally got an email that said, 'Joss gives his blessing, but he cannot speak for Fox or Universal.'"

Fisher adds, "Fox and Universal seemed to be fine with it, because we're non-profit and we're not making any

❖ Opposite top: A new ship, a new crew. The cast of the non-profit fan-film *Browncoats: Redemption*.

❖ Opposite center, top to bottom: Adam Baldwin, Mark A. Sheppard (aka Badger), Ron Glass and Michael Fairman (Niska) show their support for *Browncoats: Redemption*'s charity fund-raising aims.

❖ Opposite bottom: The feature length fan-documentary *Done the Impossible*.

❖ Above: Filming a ship's galley scene for *Browncoats: Redemption*.

money from it. All of it goes to charity [and] it gives awareness and continued support for their original properties."

Browncoats have been intensely supportive of *Redemption*, Fisher says. "As of this date, we've had a 153 people donate their time for 200 different jobs on the film. So in terms of the crew, a lot of professionals who've been in the industry were involved in this and have brought their talents to it, and all the actors have waived any fee to do the film. It's been quite a humbling experience."

Where did all those Browncoats come from? "Besides the love of the fans," Dougherty replies, "social media – Twitter, Facebook and YouTube – have been our lifeblood."

"People came from all over the country on their own dime to be extras," Fisher relates. "It was like the biggest shindig you've ever seen."

Heather Fagan, who stars as Captain Laura Matthews, is one of the people who pulled multiple duties. "I was a Browncoat before," she says. "I've actually known Mike for years and he sent me the script, just kind of, 'Hey, I'm writing this, what do you think?' 'I really like that. I want to audition for this!' He made me go through the audition process. I told him, 'I will be involved in this in any way, shape or form.' So I was a jack-of-all-trades on the set occasionally, everything from supplying food to being in front of the camera, for fifteen hours a day."

The film was shot with the digital Red One camera. "That gave us a level of production quality that's a cinema level of film," Fisher relates.

Fisher reckons that the out-of-pocket cost of *Browncoats: Redemption* is just under $30,000, with approximately another $100,000 in in-kind donations. "We've had donations from Neo Effects, who donated about $70,000 worth of CGI. Jones Soda is sponsoring the film."

Browncoats: Redemption was shot in Maryland. "Frontier Town in Ocean City donated a Western theme park for three weekends," Dougherty says.

❖ Top: Filming an ship's interior scene.

❖ Above: Shooting a fight scene at Frontier Town.

"Saint John's Properties donated their warehouse space for four months where we could build our ship. The city of Bowie donated a state park where we could film our Alliance scenes. Everything was donated because of the non-profit aspect."

With the film scheduled to premiere at Dragon Con in Atlanta in Fall 2010, there are five charities that are intended beneficiaries of any funds raised from DVD sales of *Browncoats: Redemption*: Equality Now, Kids Need to Read, the Dyslexia Foundation, the Al Wooten Jr Heritage Center and the Marine Corps and Law Enforcement Foundation. "These are charities that are actually on the ground doing stuff and affecting people," Fisher says. "If we could accomplish our goal of 32,000 units over the course of a year, then we'll definitely move forward on any sequels. I'm just humbled by everybody who's come to the table to be a part of this."

"If we accomplish our goal," Dougherty says, "we'll have reached close to half a million dollars. That's about $90,000 for each charity, and for a charity like Kids Need to Read, that's life-changing. It's Browncoats doing what they do best, which is making a difference in people's lives."

❖ Above: Two views of Neo f/x's CG model of the new ship, Redemption. CG model by Dustin Elmore, original design by Alex Bradley.

ON 'ARIEL'

Hello, everyone –

I've been asked by our cyberfriends at Fox to pitch in with an article detailing how 'Ariel' came to life. So here I am. About to detail.

Cairo, 1843. Wait, that's wrong.

Santa Monica, September of 2002. Yeah, that's better. To quote a famous dead guy, I was nervous. Very, very dreadfully nervous. I'd been a fan of *Buffy* and *Angel* and the whole Mutant Enemy camp for years, and this was my first shot at showing the best writers in television that I didn't suck. Still waiting for confirmation on that one. Um... guys?

So, it started with an idea from Joss: he wanted to do a story where Simon hired the crew for a heist. The rest was up for grabs. But since the folks around the office didn't take kindly to my random grabbing, I decided it was best for everyone if I worked at home.

After approaching the story from a few different angles, the staff and I finally landed on a take we liked. I pitched it to executive producer Tim Minear, who in typical Tim fashion said, "That's great! What else ya got?" He was kidding. (I think.) We spent the next couple of days hammering out the details, then rolled on over to the Paramount lot to pitch our ideas to Joss, who was in the middle of playing spin the bottle with David Boreanaz. Or he was directing 'Spin the Bottle' for *Angel*, I get confused. He said something along the lines of "me like" and producer Ben Edlund and I trucked back to our Santa Monica offices to put the finishing touches on the outline. At around 1:30 that morning, we finished the outline and cracked a celebratory beverage. I think Ben enjoyed it more than I did because he was laughing on his way out the door; it might have had something to do with the four days I had to write the script. He'd recently written 'Jaynestown' in about that amount of time and he was anticipating how much fun I was about to have. That must have been it, right?

So I spent four crazy days writing constantly, cursing

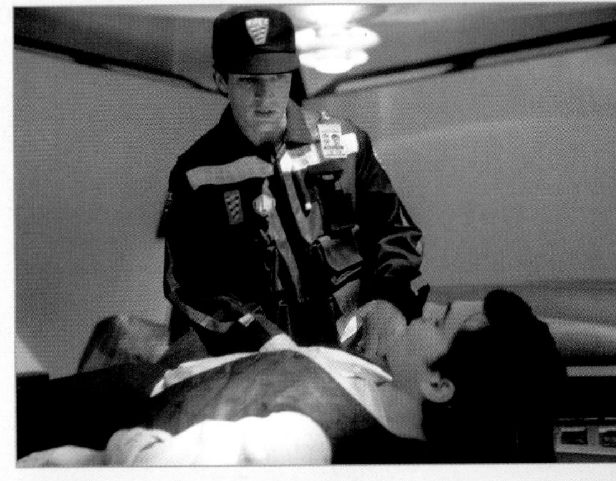

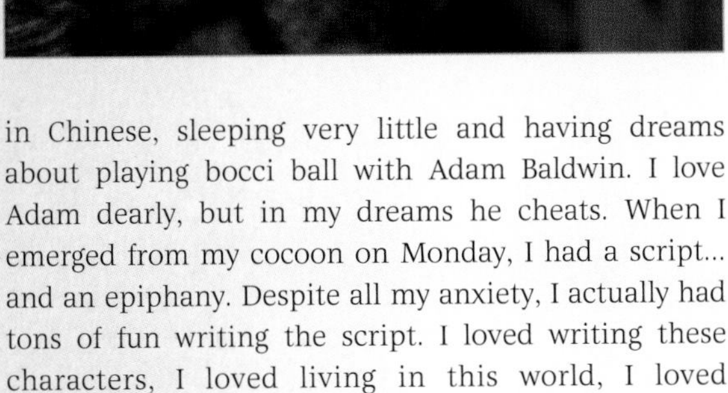

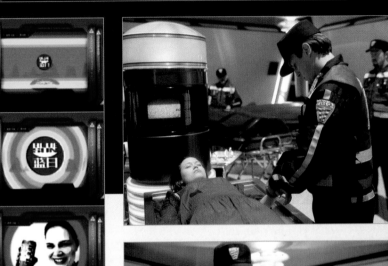

in Chinese, sleeping very little and having dreams about playing bocci ball with Adam Baldwin. I love Adam dearly, but in my dreams he cheats. When I emerged from my cocoon on Monday, I had a script... and an epiphany. Despite all my anxiety, I actually had tons of fun writing the script. I loved writing these characters, I loved living in this world, I loved everything. YOU GUYS! (sniff)

I also loved being done! And watching as the best cast and crew in town turned the pretty pictures in my head into reality was a blast. I'm extremely grateful and indebted to everyone who worked their gluteal regions off to make this episode as cool as it is. It's a bit of a departure – we have a Core planet, sonic rifles, and some big bad villains swooping in to complicate things. It's sort of *Ocean's Eleven* meets *The X-Files* in space. Or *Curse of the Mummy* meets *The A-Team*. Also heavily influenced by *Chico and the Man*. All right, I don't know. Just watch it and you can tell me.

I hope you enjoy the show as much as we enjoyed making it. I think you will!

ORIGINALLY PUBLISHED ON FOX.COM, 2002

TAKE THE SKY

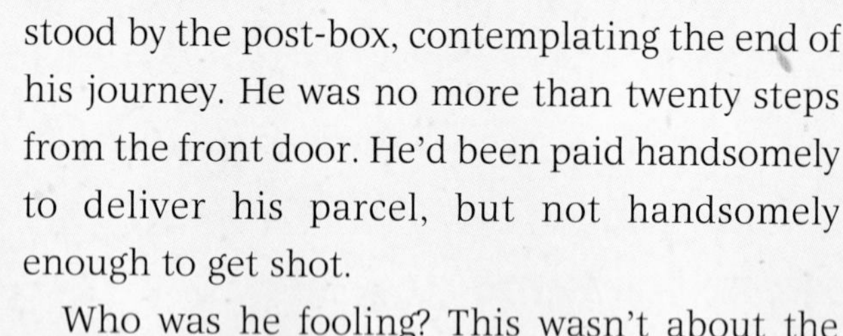

// BY JOSE MOLINA

The handwritten scrawl on the post-box read "Reynolds". A few steps past, the sign before the porch read "Trespassers Will Be Shot." Beyond, inked in red, a final warning was scratched out on the waterlogged wood of the front door.

"NO, SERIOUSLY."

Fist-sized shotgun blasts in the wood confirmed the truth of the message.

The small, wooden house sat on a remote mesa, and a gangly kid with a dust-streaked face stood by the post-box, contemplating the end of his journey. He was no more than twenty steps from the front door. He'd been paid handsomely to deliver his parcel, but not handsomely enough to get shot.

Who was he fooling? This wasn't about the delivery, or the parcel, or the pay. It was about getting a first-hand look at Malcolm Reynolds.

The kid girded himself, approached the door and raised his hand to knock. The door swung open before his knuckles landed.

"Ni dao di yao shen me?"

The kid looked up at Reynolds. He was taller than expected. Broader. His eyes bore into the young man like a fishhook, and immediately he understood why some men followed Reynolds to their grave while others strove to dig him one.

The kid was staring, and he knew it. Seventy-odd years had carved Reynolds' face with countless stories, and he wanted to hear every one of them. Especially the ones about the countless slingers who'd thought they could take out the one and only Malco—

"Spit it out." The voice snapped the kid back to reality, and he extended his hands for the old man to see the parcel he'd brought.

"P-post for you, sir."

Reynolds eyed the box — a long, thin object — then took it and swiped his thumb across the kid's ident scanner before stepping back and reaching for his door.

"S-scuse me, sir —" the kid interrupted before the door shut. "I was curious about some—"

"Make up your own story," said Reynolds.

He slammed the door shut.

Mal ripped into the package as he walked into what passed for his living room: a chair, a vidscreen, a collection of mostly empty bottles, a rack of mostly loaded weapons. He didn't receive much mail out here on the rim; few people knew where to find him, and those few knew to leave him be unless there was trouble. So what kind of trouble did this small box spell?

He pulled the contents out one at a time: a note, a vidstrip, and an oblong velvet box. A jewelry box. Curiosity scratched at the back of Mal's brain, but he didn't believe in opening presents on Christmas Eve. He'd leave the box for last, and start with the note.

It was from Zoe.

"Jayne stole this. Thought you'd want it back."

Eight words. Sounded like Zoe. She didn't talk much these days. She spent too much time out in the black with no one to talk to. The last time she and Mal had spoken was two years back, when she'd brought Serenity home for a visit.

A pang of jealousy had shot through him when he saw his old boat, but it was Zoe's home now, not his. She needed it more than Mal did. It no longer afforded Mal the anonymity he craved anyway. The ship was synonymous with "The Signal." With galaxy-shattering heroics no one man could or should have to embody. Once upon a time, Serenity had been a place of refuge for Mal. It was no longer that for him. It could still be that for Zoe.

Let her have the sky. They'd taken it from him.

Mal passed his finger across the vidstrip, sparking it to life. Why Zoe would think him interested in a news vid was beyond his comprehension, but he'd give her the benefit of the doubt. If he found a single story about himself, however, he'd have to wave her with some words.

But the story she wanted Mal to see wasn't about him. It was about Jayne.

"BILLIONAIRE COBB FOUND DEAD IN BED," was the headline. Exactly as Jayne would've wanted, thought Mal. Then he played the rest of the story, and laughed for the first time in weeks.

After the events at Mr. Universe's complex, Jayne had been the only one to embrace celebrity. For Mal, fame brought questions he didn't want to answer, scrutiny that he would not abide. For Jayne, being a hero meant money. It meant women. It meant respect. Yes, it also caused a lifetime of rats to skitter from the proverbial woodwork, but whatever bygones he couldn't buy he could mostly achieve via shooting, stabbing or garroting.

"BILLIONAIRE COBB FOUND DEAD IN BED." Mal expected a story of debauchery to follow — four women, a weeklong binge, several broken laws of both man and nature. Instead, a sober-faced journalist reported the reality.

Apparently, after being booted from a half-dozen watering holes the night before he was found, Jayne returned home alone and collapsed in bed from a combination of exhaustion and drink. As usual, he took his beloved Vera to bed with him.

The reporter proceeded to explain — with a solemnity that plainly masked her embarrassment — how Jayne appeared to

BILLIONAIRE COBB FOUND DEAD IN BED

CLEAR SIGNALS

mistake his semi-automatic rifle for a woman... whether in his sleep or inebriation... and accidentally shot himself in the neck. Twice.

Mal set aside the vidstrip and picked up the jewelry box. Jayne stole this from him? Mal couldn't recall ever owning jewelry, especially not the kind that came in a fancy velvet box. That was Inara's stock in trade. He shook the name from his mind and opened the box. Inside was a silver crucifix; he hadn't worn it since the Independents' defeat at Serenity Valley.

It all made sense now. Mal could never bring himself to dispose of the crucifix. Jayne could never bring himself to sell it. Neither would've been able to explain why, nor would they have accepted another's explanation. Jayne's simple truth was that he feared "gettin' smote." Mal's less-simple truth was that the cross was a token — an emblem. Not of Salvation or whatever other nonsense got peddled in the Fat Book or any assortment of lesser-known fat books. It was a token of hope. It had nothing to do with religion, or faith, or God, but simple symbolism. Mal could live without a lot, but not without hope... or, at the very least, the hope of hope.

It was that same hope that had always kept him going back to Inara. Hope that she'd one day turn her back on her vocation and ask him to lay down his guns and his burdens. A normal life with the most extraordinary woman he'd ever met — that was worth holding out hope.

The problem with hope was that the rug-pull was always all the more painful when it came. And it always came. Mal should've known better; if he expected nothing, then something was a pleasant surprise. If he hoped for something...

...he put it out of his mind. He'd gone over this enough to know where it led. Both he and Inara would've endured far less if they'd gone on their merry. And now there was no going back.

Mal forced himself to think happy thoughts. Kittens and bunnies, gorramit. Big fat babies. That was better. Big fat babies. Violet and Caleb Tam. They were far from babies anymore, but that was still how Mal chose to remember them — the way they looked when Mal last visited Kaylee and Simon on Ariel.

Violet took after her mother. She was a sweet, kind little soul who exhibited heaps of confusion during the inevitable occasions when she made little Caleb cry. No matter how many times Kaylee asked her not to take apart his toys to see how they worked, little Violet couldn't help herself. The three year-old spent most of Mal's last visit trying to increase the nav-thrust on Caleb's tri-mobile by replacing its battery-powered motor with an internal combustion engine. Caleb spent most of the visit on his mother's lap.

The boy definitely took after his father. He was far tougher than he looked. Smart as a whip and stubborn as the day was long. He'd go to bed only when he was tired, not because Kaylee "said so." He couldn't be convinced that it was beneficial to sleep at any time other than when one was, in fact, sleepy. Only Simon could get little Caleb to bed with the promise of reading him some doorstop of a book.

Ultimately, though, both kids had as much of River in them as they did their own parents. After all, it was River who spent the most time with them, sitting for the twins any time of day or night to accommodate for Simon and Kaylee's busy Cityfolk schedules.

And the twins loved their Auntie River. She'd hold cockroach races for them and tell them which one was going to win before they even started. She'd tell hour-long stories that would literally hypnotize them and make them believe they were part of the tale. She'd clean up scrapes with such vivid descriptions of the gruesome wars being waged by microscopic organisms inside their tiny bodies that the twins would forget the pain in lieu of being nauseous.

If Simon was brain and Kaylee was heart, then River was spirit. The Tam family was a confluence of all good things, and it eased Mal's weary mind to think of them on some distant place far, far away from his desolate rock.

At his age, Mal often found himself lost in musings. He didn't know how much longer he'd have to wait for a grave to call his own, but he knew he'd done a lot of living in his years. He would die alone. Here, in this box of sticks he called a house. None of his remaining friends would attend his funeral, simply because weeks would go by before they heard of his passing.

It was how it had to be.

He'd come to terms with all that. Mal had lost a lot. Sacrificed a lot. Happiness had visited him rarely in his waning years, the quiet and the stillness of age replacing the chaotic commotion of his youth.

But Mal was lonely. Very lonely out here on the rim.

It was how it had to be.

It had been his decision. He'd come to terms with that, too.

But this — the here and now — is no time for musings. This is time to act.

Mal stands before The Operative.

He's mere steps from the console that will allow him to broadcast the Parliament's sins to the entire 'verse. The people will know the truth...

"...'cause they need to," Mal tells The Operative.

"Do you really believe that?" asks The Operative.

"I do."

"You willing to die for that belief?"

Mal stops to think. He is willing to die for that belief. Dying is easy. Living is hard.

But is Mal willing to *live* with the decision he's about to make? To forever alter the course of his life, for better or — most like — for worse. To become, in the eyes of the 'verse, something he's not: a savior.

But no man can know the future. Mal can only *hope*.

He lets the same principles that have always guided him dictate his choice. It's not about what's best for him. It's about what's best, period.

"I am," says Mal, unwavering.

The Operative nods his understanding. He and Captain Reynolds may have different worldviews, but The Operative can't help respecting the man's convictions. That is, until he starts shooting.

"'course, that ain't exactly Plan A."

MUTANT ENEMIES?

Some closing words...

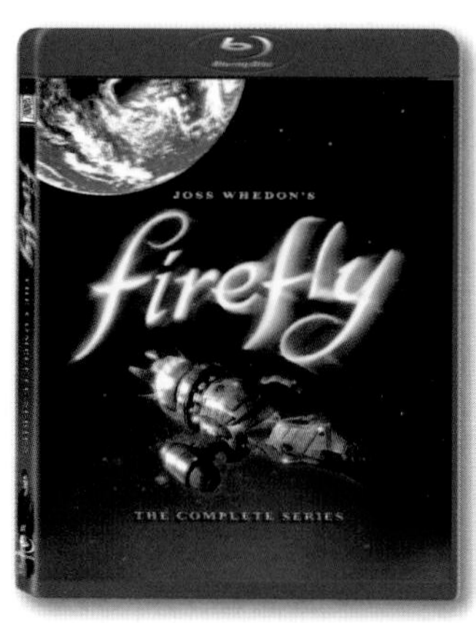

In 2008, Joss Whedon, Nathan Fillion, Alan Tudyk and Ron Glass reunited to record a roundtable discussion for inclusion as a bonus extra on the *Firefly* Blu-ray set. There was a lot of laughter. Here's an excerpt, where Whedon discusses a script idea he had back in 2002:

Joss: I wanted to do – was dead serious about doing – monster cattle... And the way I was going to justify monster cattle was the idea that they didn't send animals to the distant planets, they'd send DNA scrip, you know, "Here's the test tube, you grow your own." And it went *badly*... so we were going to have monsters. We had a telepathic girl... so I felt we could get away with a little mutation stuff.

Alan: But Cows?

Joss: But cows are my favorite. Probably I would have been talked into something else.

Nathan: Monkeys!

Joss: Well, horses, because then, you know, the executives who said, "Why are there horses?" and it would be [makes mutant horse noises] ripping people apart and stuff, "That's why there's horses! 'Cause they're *awesome*!"
[Pause.]
Or they could be *bad* horses. Nah, we would never do that...